JOSSEY-BASS™
A Wiley Brand

Courting the Wealthy

SECOND EDITION

Scott C. Stevenson, Editor

WILEY

Courting the Wealthy

— 2nd Edition —

Published by

Stevenson, Inc.

P.O. Box 4528 • Sioux City, Iowa • 51104

Phone 712.239.3010 • Fax 712.239.2166

www.stevensoninc.com

Table of Contents

Table of Contents

Systems & Procedures for Managing the Cultivation Process

The process of identifying major gift prospects and building relationships that moves them toward the realization of major gifts should be systematic. "Moves management," a term coined by nationally-recognized consultant Jerold Panas, involves both highly-personalized and "broad-brush" actions aimed at securing major gifts. To properly manage and track the cultivation several or even dozens of prospects, it's important to have a useful system and set of procedures in place.

Every Call Has Its Purpose

Does every call you make have a clear-cut objective? It should.

Whether you're making a face-to-face call on a prospect, a phone call to a donor or directing a letter to a foundation official, all prospect/donor calls should have clear objectives in mind.

As you identify objectives prior to each call, determine the degree to which they will move the prospect closer to the realization of a gift.

Here are some examples of objectives you may want to accomplish:

- To thank the donor for his/her gift.
- To invite the prospect's participation.
- To introduce your organization and its programs to a new prospect.
- To cultivate the prospect closer to the realization of a major gift.
- To invite a prospect to join a committee as a way to cultivate his/her interest and realize an eventual major gift.
- To begin to reverse the prospect's negative attitude toward your charity.

Include your objectives in your written post-visit, call or trip report.

Today's Cultivations are Tomorrow's Realized Gifts

As a nonprofit's capital campaign nears, staff members often realize they don't have sufficient prospects to garner the size and number of major gifts needed to establish a lofty campaign goal. That's why you can never identify and cultivate too many individuals, businesses and foundations.

It helps to fully understand that the earnest identification, research and cultivation you do today will materialize into generous gifts down the road — when you decide to embark on a major asset-building program.

Just as it's important to set annual dollar goals, be sure to also establish quantifiable objectives that address:

- Number of new prospects identified quarterly/yearly.
- Number of cultivation moves per prospect per year.
- Number of personal cultivation visits per week/month.
- Number of prospect profiles completed.
- Number of rating/screening sessions held per quarter.
- Number of volunteers assisting with identification, research and cultivation.

Choose From Menu of Cultivation Moves

Cultivation moves represent actions designed to bring prospects closer to the realization of a major gift.

Each move can be measured. The moves should be planned in your eyes, but should appear unplanned and spontaneous to the prospect.

To plan appropriate moves for each prospect at each point of cultivation, develop a list of actions from which to draw. In fact, develop two lists: One that includes individual cultivation moves and another oriented toward group cultivation.

Here are examples of both:

Individual Cultivation Moves

- ❑ A personal note from your board chair.
- ❑ Using the prospect's home or office to host a reception.
- ❑ A profile article in your newsletter or magazine.
- ❑ An introduction at a board meeting.
- ❑ A request for advice.
- ❑ Special mementos or letters of thanks for past acts.
- ❑ An invitation to join a committee or your board.
- ❑ Dinner with your CEO.
- ❑ Awards based on various criteria.
- ❑ A request for assistance based on the prospect's business or talents.

Group Cultivation Moves

- ❑ Participation in a golf classic.
- ❑ Inclusion in your list of annual contributors.
- ❑ Receiving your newsletter or magazine.
- ❑ Receiving a holiday greeting card.
- ❑ Inclusion in group receptions.
- ❑ Inclusion in a specific gift club.
- ❑ Participation in a particular reunion.
- ❑ Inclusion in a group survey.

Formulate Written Yearly Major Gifts Plan to Create Goals, Measurable Outcomes

Creating and following a written plan to bring in major gifts is the only no-fail way to ensure your organization will get these necessary donations, especially in a slumping economy.

Laura Fredericks, planning and fundraising consultant, learned the value of written major gifts plans early in her career as a fundraiser for a variety of organizations, including six years as vice president of philanthropy at Pace University (New York, NY), where having a written plan helped her bring in $92 million for the school.

"Right now, the more structure and the more concrete ways you can develop priorities and benchmarks, the better off you'll be," Fredericks says. "Gone are the days of the great cause. People don't give money just because they like you anymore."

Major gifts are also becoming the most dependable source of income for nonprofits, with nearly 80 percent of the $307 billion given to nonprofits in the United States in 2008 coming from individuals, she notes.

Fredericks shares a generic major gifts plan below and shares how to turn major gifts prospects into donors in the story at right.

Source: Laura Fredericks, Consultant, Laura Fredericks, New York, NY. Phone (212) 929-9120. E-mail: lauradashfredericks@gmail.com

Content not available in this edition

Turn Major Gifts Prospects Into Donors

Major gifts fundraising consultant Laura Fredericks (New York, NY) says that identifying potential donors of major gifts is only half the battle of realizing major gifts. You also have to convince them to give.

Here, Fredericks outlines steps on how to turn those prospects into major donors for your cause:

☐ **Get your team together:** A few months before your new fiscal year, set a budget meeting for staff members most involved with fundraising. Have your information technology staff provide useful statistics and reports related to past donations so you have all the information you need to plan realistically.

☐ **Make the budget:** Keeping in mind projects you would like to complete in the next few years, make three budgets: one with less money than this year, one with more, and one with the same amount. This helps you prepare for some funding not coming through. Any significant amounts not already taken care of through current grants or planned gifts, you probably need to raise through donors. "You can't bank on trusts and annuities coming in," she says.

☐ **Write down objectives:** As outlined in the generic major gifts plan, at left, create and take concrete steps to reach your fundraising goal. Put your organization's plan in writing and give copies to everyone involved.

☐ **Create responsibility:** Delegating duties to all staff and board members, even select volunteers, for major gift fundraising is the most important — but often the most neglected — part of meeting goals, Fredericks says. Make sure everyone understands what is expected of him or her. "We're all in it together, and it's important to have ownership, to be vested in the outcome," she says.

☐ **Do double duty:** Prime time for major gift recruitment is when people are least busy — typically mid-September to early December and mid-January to mid-May. Many organizations already do special events during those months, which tends to take away from concentration on other things. But you can make every event a major gift event, Fredericks says. Know whom you want to see at the event, invite them, seat them next to key staffers or volunteers, and follow up.

☐ **Track progress monthly:** If you don't, you probably won't meet your goal, she says. You'll need to adjust your plan accordingly if you are not on track to raise as much money as you'd like. When goals are not met, have the person responsible for meeting that goal write a short description of why they were not able to meet them.

Form Provides Snapshot of Cultivation Activity

Although various forms and software allow you to track individual prospect cultivation activities — specific actions that move a prospect closer to the realization of making a major gift — the form shown here offers a simple snapshot of a group of prospects over a six-month period. This provides a way to visually compare cultivation among prospects and identify any deficits in individual prospect attention.

The form can be used by individual development officers in charge of managing a specified number of gift prospects and can also be used by those whose job it is to supervise development officers' cultivation activities.

The person completing the cultivation form can use this tool to plan individual cultivation strategies, to keep a record of each cultivation move as it occurs and to evaluate past cultivation activity.

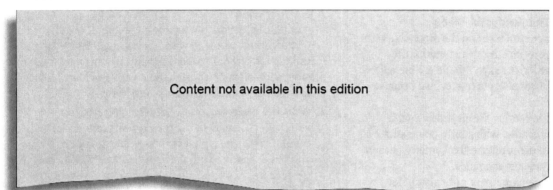

Simply list top prospects' names in the left column, then fill in the date and type of cultivation taking place: face-to-face visit (V), visit by the prospect to your facilities (F), written correspondence (C) or phone call (P).

Track Your Top 50 Corporate Prospects

As important as it is to track cultivation/solicitation activity of individual prospects, it's equally important to track top corporate prospects. And because key activities surrounding corporate prospects can differ from those for individuals, using software or a form such as the example shown here is a useful tool for corporate gifts managers.

First, identify and prioritize your top 50 corporate prospects by reviewing past donor files, conducting rating and screening sessions among staff, board members and other volunteers and by other means.

Once you identify your top 50 corporate prospects based on capability and inclination to give, plan and monitor all cultivation and solicitation moves monthly. This collective view of activities surrounding your top 50 will help in the overall solicitation of these key prospects.

Create and utilize a form such as this to track top corporate prospects.

Identify, Cultivate Prospects Between Capital Campaigns

If you've just finished a capital campaign or are years from launching one, it's the perfect time to produce and follow a written prospect identification and cultivation plan. This plan will put in place strategies designed to expand your prospect pool and begin a massive cultivation process.

Make these key elements part of your written plan to identify, research and cultivate major gift prospects:

1. **Have a stewardship plan for past donors.** Recognize that all past donors will be your best candidates for repeat major gifts. Craft individualized stewardship actions for each donor. Retention is the name of the game if you want to expand, not simply replace, your donor pool.

2. **Identify new, capable prospects.** Establish procedures that identify and prioritize new prospects based on financial capability and inclination to give to your cause. Make these procedures part of your three- to five-year plan.

3. **Manage an ongoing cultivation plan.** Develop tailored cultivation strategies for each of your prospects. Recognize that the person responsible for managing the plan may not, in many or most instances, be the one responsible for carrying out individual cultivation moves. Know that each move should bring each prospect closer to the realization of an eventual major gift.

Form Provides Helpful Way to Monitor Activity

All too often, procrastination and other distractions prevent development personnel from carrying out those functions that are most critical — making regular contact with prospects and donors.

Recording that activity weekly helps to reinforce its importance among all involved.

If you manage others who are responsible for calling on prospects and donors as a part of their responsibilities, it's important to have them regularly record their activity.

Why? For several reasons. First, doing so helps them more accurately analyze how their time is being spent. Second, it helps you, as the manager, monitor how their time is being used. And finally, the written report provides a lasting record that can be used to improve effectiveness as you plan subsequent years' goals and objectives.

Whether staff track cultivation and solicitation activity via computer software, their PDA or with a simple pen and notebook, the report should include the kinds of information provided on the weekly calls report depicted below.

Content not available in this edition

Educate and Train Fellow Employees

Time and effort invested in educating employees outside your development office about major gifts can pay off big through their willingness to identify, cultivate, steward and even help solicit major gifts.

Here are ideas to get your fellow employees more involved in major gifts efforts:

✓ Distribute a twice-monthly e-newsletter or memo to employees sharing what is happening in your office with regard to major gifts: details of funding opportunities, summaries of recent gifts, mention of events they can attend and more.

✓ Ask them to accompany you on calls. There's no better

teacher than experience. Their participation will only serve to energize them.

✓ Spoon-feed tasks with which they can help: sharing names, rating and screening prospects, identifying potential funding opportunities and more.

✓ Celebrate and recognize all levels of participation. Keep employees updated on any progress on a prospect with whom they have had any level of involvement; make your other employees aware of their involvement.

Recognize that nurturing employees takes time, just as it does with board members and other volunteers, but know also that your investment of time will pay off.

A Simple Spreadsheet Can Boost Donor Relations

When Angela Townsend became development director at Tabby's Place (Ringoes, NJ) in mid-2008, she quickly realized one of her most important tasks would be to reach out to each donor — large or small — because all are important to the small nonprofit.

"Our donors kind of expect that," Townsend says of the regular recognition. "It's like expecting personal service from a small mom-and-pop shop."

As the organization's sole development staff person, Townsend looked to organize and streamline these outreach efforts to make them more effective.

Using Microsoft Excel, she created a simple but specific spreadsheet that allows her to keep meticulous track of every form of contact with each donor.

The form, Townsend says, "is extremely simple ... and it has become what sets us apart from other organizations."

The development director's spreadsheet consists of five columns that contain:

1. The name of any donor who has made a one-time donation of $100 or more, as well as every regular monthly donor.

2. Space for Townsend to make personal notes to help jog her memory about the donor.

3. Phone numbers for the donor.

4. The date of the last contact Townsend or one of her volunteers had with that donor.

5. Information on what that contact was (e.g., phone call, in-person visit, mailed card).

By sorting the list by the dates in the fourth column, Townsend can easily see who's gone the longest without a contact.

"We try not to let anybody go more than three months without a contact from us," she says, "like a card with photos, a thoughtful note or just a hello and an open call to invite them to come in and see what's going on and what's new." While Townsend was originally handling all of these donor relations by herself, she now regularly uses two volunteers to help write notes and make calls.

The success has been tangible, Townsend says. "Very frequently after one of these outreaches, we get a nice check from one of these folks. And about 20 of our donors have commented specifically that this affection and attention is unlike anything they've ever experienced with any nonprofit before."

Source: Angela Townsend, Director of Development, Tabby's Place, Ringoes, NJ. Phone (908) 237-5300. E-mail: info@tabbysplace.org

This sample Microsoft Excel document illustrates the simple-yet-effective way Angela Townsend, director of development at Tabby's Place (Ringoes, NJ), manages donor contacts.

Content not available in this edition

Courting the Wealthy, Second Edition.
Edited by Scott C. Stevenson.
© 2010 Stevenson, Inc. Published 2010 by Stevenson, Inc.

The Empathy Factor: Keying In on Donors' Wants, Needs

Too many charities focus on their own set of wants and needs rather than those of the donor. The development shops that achieve the highest level of major gifts success include those where their focus is on the donor. Empathy, good listening skills and a sensitivity to donors' wants and needs are key to achieving success.

Listen for Prospects' Cues

As you meet with prospective donors, listen for cues that provide clear opportunities to make your case.

Here are some examples of prospect cues that merit an immediate response:

"I've always thought more should be done to maintain and enhance our community's parks and green spaces."

"It's too bad there aren't many tax incentives for charitable gifts."

"Why isn't more being done to prepare young people for careers in.... ?"

Understand Your Prospect

People will always look at the cost-to-benefit ratio once they've decided how much to contribute. Knowing that fact in advance — as well as other unique characteristics of each donor — will help you anticipate where to best focus your efforts.

Seven Ways to Make Donors Comfortable Enough to Give

To build major donors, you must first build trust between your organization and prospects. To strengthen that relationship:

1. **Have a donor bill of rights.** Post it where visitors can see it. Send a copy of it out, along with a thank-you note, to first-time donors.

2. **Follow up with first-time donors.** Make a call to that first-time donor to say thank you and find out why he/she chose you.

3. **Make sure the money goes where it's meant to go.** Ensure that restricted gifts go where they are supposed to and share information with donors about that (e.g., if donation is to fund summer camp programs, send photos out once camp is over).

4. **Be specific.** Go to donors with specific needs, not just asking for general donations.

5. **Meet face-to-face.** At least once a year, find a way to get in front of significant donors. Host a brunch with the CEO, have a VIP reception or offer to visit them at home.

6. **Make thank-you calls.** Donors like to hear from you, especially when you're not asking for money. Calling to say thanks or to ask their opinion on a new project or program shows that you feel their investment in your organization goes beyond their donations.

7. **Be thoughtful.** Consider why donors might make a gift to your organization. Also, think about what might keep them from making one.

Know When to Hit the Brakes

You've met with a prospective donor several times to build a relationship and begin to explore funding opportunities. Each time you have felt positive about the progress being made. But this time was different. The prospect showed more hesitation about considering a major gift. What to do?

This is the when some development professionals get anxious, and instead of slowing down, hit the accelerator and push for a gift. That's the wrong approach.

If you meet with a "probable donor" — a term coined by philanthropic consultant Jerold Panas — who seems hesitant or reluctant, slow down. Give the person room to breathe.

If the person feels pressure, the chance of a gift will quickly diminish.

Rather than push for a commitment, pinpoint the hesitancy. Ask a probing question. The issue may simply be a matter of timing, or perhaps the donor's funding interests are different than what you perceived them to be. Then leave on a positive note and agree to meet again.

Recognize that the final decision to make a major gift needs to come from within. After all, your goal should be to protect and nurture a long-term relationship that may result in multiple gifts and perhaps even a planned gift over time.

To Make the Most of Naming Opportunities, Let Donor Drive

Naming opportunities are one of the most successful fundraising tools, allowing organizations to provide a built-in stewardship service with little additional overhead.

Lynnie Meyer, executive director of the Children's Hospital Foundation and Norton Healthcare Foundation (Louisville, KY), says that truly successful naming programs require a balanced and multi-faceted approach. In pursuing naming gifts, Meyer says:

- ❑ **Let your donor guide you.** Like any fundraising activity, naming opportunities begin with the personal relationship between you and your donor. Let donors decide on the area they are interested in giving, how gifts will be structured, and how they want to receive recognition — an announcement at a public event, anonymity? Do they want to give a gift outright, or put it into a larger project fund? "The anatomy of the gift will emerge," Meyer says. "It's all about donor intention and meeting the needs of the donor." Know also that there is more to a naming opportunity than the name itself: Donors should feel a connection and sense of ownership over projects they are funding. Personalized naming projects can foster larger donations than a fixed naming opportunity and will keep donors closely connected to your organization.

- ❑ **Be specific.** Share public lists of needs and their recognition opportunities; even if donors are interested in unlisted projects, a list will promote a sense of urgency and idea of cost involved. At Norton, donors can endow a fellowship for $270,000; smaller donations of $4,000 to $5,000 endow professorships. For facility projects, Meyer suggests advertising naming opportunities at about 50 percent of overall cost (e.g., if building will cost $20 million, a donor can name it for a $10 million commitment).

- ❑ **Be flexible.** "(The hospital's needs) are a moving target," Meyer says, "so our list of naming opportunities is updated as projects develop." Once donors choose a point of interest, walk them through a unit or show them a blueprint, and refine from there.

- ❑ **Keep it visible.** Meyer and her team keep a list of potential naming opportunities online "to keep visibility high and help people recognize we are still in a campaign." Additionally, donor packets for the foundations include a separate insert that highlights naming opportunities, plus a pledge card. "Once we are engaging donors at that level," Meyer says, "we already have an ongoing relationship with them. The naming opportunity allows us to say thank you."

Source: Lynnie Meyer, Executive Director, Children's Hospital Foundation and Norton Healthcare Foundation, Louisville, KY. Phone (502) 629-8060. E-mail: lynnie.meyer@nortonhealth.org. Website: www.nortonhealthcare.org

Factors Donors Want to Know

Before writing a check, most potential donors want to be assured their money is going to a worthwhile, well-run cause. Taking steps to inform them of this up front can streamline the gift process and boost the number and amount of gifts received.

Levé (Portland, OR) is a six-year-old nonprofit that supports other local charitable groups by doing fundraising on their behalf. Kiernan Doherty, president, shares six key elements her board looks for when deciding to fund a specific charity:

1. **A new and specific program or initiative Levé's funds would allow the organization to implement.** "We look for organizations that will be greatly impacted by our contribution," she says.

2. **Well-kept financials, past and present.** "Show you're financially stable enough that we can guarantee you'll still be operating at the end of the year," Doherty says. Any major donor is going to be savvy with money; show them that you are, too.

3. **A primary point of contact throughout the donation process.** This shows you're not all volunteer run, and that you're also not someone's pet project. This is also good customer service. A potential donor should be handled by one person from your organization, should have that person's contact information, and should feel confident that person personally knows him/her.

4. **Board opportunities.** Levé looks for volunteer opportunities for its board members so donors feel personally connected to that organization, not just there when it's short on funds.

5. **Environmentally sustainable practices.** Even if your mission does not concern the environment, sustainable practices (recycling, etc.) show you think progressively and treat others conscientiously.

6. **An organization that is not bigger than the gift itself.** You don't want a donor thinking that his or her donation "means very little to your organization," Doherty says. It can lead to less engagement and less passion on both sides of the equation.

Source: Kiernan Doherty, President, Levé, Portland, OR. Phone (503) 320-7076. E-mail: kdoherty@metgroup.com. Website: www.leve-nw.org

The Empathy Factor: Keying In On Donors' Wants , Needs

Know Your USPs

Sales professionals call them USPs: unique selling points.

What are your nonprofit's USPs? What distinguishes your organization from the competition? A mission unlike any other? A volunteer corps that contributes thousands of hours a year? A 100-year history of feeding the community's hungry?

To capture the attention of would-be donors, it's important to identify your USPs and use them to make a compelling case for support.

Listen for What Matters

- If your prospect brings up a point more than once, that generally means the point is significant to him/her.

Share Heroic Anecdotes

What do you do when you hear of a major gift that benefited some other charity?

Share such transformational gift examples with board members and others capable of making similar gifts to your organization. Hero stories about persons who made significant gifts can positively influence your own constituency and nurture inclinations to do the same.

Whether you send an occasional news clipping or distribute a regular list of your community's major gifts/donors to a select group of constituents, the persistent tap, tap, tap of major gift information will keep this topic at the forefront and move them to make gifts of their own.

Go a step further: Identify a nonprofit that received a major gift a year or so ago. Ask how the gift has impacted the organization and those it serves and other ways it has transformed the organization. Report these findings to your own would-be donors. Such examples will also help encourage and motivate similar gifts for your own charity.

Learn to Inspire Others

Major gifts are often the result of having been inspired by someone.

Are you familiar with how to inspire others? Use any of these methods to inspire prospects with whom you come in contact and to develop methods unique to your organization:

- ❑ **To achieve greatness:** "The successful completion of this campaign will place us in the top 10 percent of our nation's colleges."

- ❑ **To help others:** "Gifts to this effort will help to prevent birth defects and literally save lives."

- ❑ **To become a hero:** "We can think of no other individual who has the capacity to make such an impact on our institution and the lives of those we serve."

- ❑ **To be an example to others:** "Our library has yet to receive a $1 million gift. Your leadership in setting such a precedent will influence others to step forward in significant ways."

- ❑ **To compete with other causes:** "Our hospital ranks midway in the nation with regard to cardiac services. The successful completion of this campaign will place us in the top five hospitals in a five-state region."

Learn the Why Behind Each Major Gift

Any time someone makes a major gift, it's important to learn why at the time the decision is made.

Getting a donor to articulate his/her decision to make a major gift during the period in which it is made has multiple benefits, including:

- Helping pinpoint, in the donor's words, exactly what motivated the gift — a tool that may help when soliciting future gifts.

- By enabling major donors to hear themselves verbalizing why they made the gift, the decision to do so becomes even more accepted.

- The act of asking donors why they are making such a significant gift is another way to demonstrate a genuine interest in them. It is an act of stewardship.

Don't hesitate to ask donors repeatedly — in different ways and at different times — why they are making such a generous gift. Most donors will welcome the opportunity to respond.

Ask Probing Questions

Here are ways to ask donors why they decided to make a major gift:

1. "We are so grateful for your generous gift. How did you ultimately arrive at that decision?"

2. "At what point did you decide this was something you wanted to do?"

3. "Was there a specific experience in your life that helped you arrive at the decision to make a major gift?"

4. "I'm always curious when someone makes a gift of this magnitude. What motivated you to do this?"

Forming First-time Relationships

Major gifts come from individuals who have both the capability to give generously and the inclination to give. Inclination to give requires some level of connection with your organization: The individual once benefited from your services or resides in the same community or has a strong belief in your organization's mission. It takes both patience and skill to form relationships with those for whom no obvious connection presently exists. Just getting your foot in the door can be challenging.

Sometimes a Letter of Introduction Is the Best Approach

When making initial contact with a new major gift prospect, involving someone familiar with both your organization and the prospect is helpful, but not always possible.

In situations where you're the only individual capable of making an introduction, begin with a sincere letter that sets the stage for an appointment. If appropriate, mention that a mutual friend suggested you contact the prospect.

Remember these four additional points as you produce a letter of introduction:

1. To the highest degree possible, tailor your letter to the prospect's interests and personality. This is where having background information is helpful.

2. Remember your primary objective: to have the opportunity to meet face-to-face.

3. Promise to limit your time to an hour or less.

4. Thank prospect(s) in advance for agreeing to meet with you.

This sample letter illustrates how to approach a prospect with whom you have no prior connection.

Caring Hands YOUTH SERVICES

September 20, 2009

Dr. and Mrs. Arthur Scott
4239 2nd Avenue North
Minneapolis, MN 55413

Dear Dr. and Mrs. Scott:

About two weeks ago your friends, Dr. and Mrs. Alan Feinstein, suggested I contact you simply to tell you about our agency and introduce you to some of what we are accomplishing throughout greater Minneapolis.

Caring Hands Youth Services was founded in 1978 to reach out to the youth of greater Minneapolis — ages 4 to 18 — as a means to nurture their God-given talents and support their families in preparing today's youth for tomorrow's challenges.

On average, Caring Hands works with some 15,000 youth on a yearly basis and has gained national recognition for some of our initiatives.

One of our more recent accomplishments, for instance, was to provide training for nearly 300 middle school children in web site development — a skill with increasing demand in this age of computer technology. And the resulting implications of this program are significant.

If you would be so kind as to give me just one hour of your time, I would like to tell you more about this and other programs and the difference they are making in the lives of our community's youth.

I will phone you within the next week to set a time and location convenient for both of you to meet. In the meantime, I thank you for your willingness to give me your attention.

Sincerely,

Megan A. Anderson
Director of Development

Caring Hands Youth Services • 1919 Lexus Avenue • Minneapolis, MN 55412

Focus on Ways to Grow Your Pool of Investors

In spite of your need for immediate major gifts, a down economy offers the perfect time to focus efforts on building new relationships with those who have the capacity to one day make a major investment in your organization. After all, if many of your existing prospects are not currently in a position to be asked for major gifts, it would be worthwhile in the long run for you and your staff to concentrate on forging relationships with those who will, down the road, include your charity at the top of their favorite causes.

To focus your efforts on creating and nurturing new relationships with financially capable individuals, businesses and foundations, develop a number of quantifiable objectives such as these:

1. To ask each board member to help identify, introduce and cultivate relationships with no fewer than three friends, relatives or associates capable of making gifts of $25,000 or more.

2. To meet with no fewer than one new prospect a week (four/month) for the purpose of introducing your charity and beginning to nurture a relationship.

3. To coordinate no fewer than two events throughout the fiscal year with the intent of attracting new (and existing) persons of wealth to attend.

4. To establish a major gifts committee and, with the committee, develop a set of quantifiable expectations that includes the identification, introduction and cultivation of new prospects throughout the fiscal year.

5. To launch a new and ongoing program that attracts the interest of local and area businesses.

6. To initiate a dialogue with no fewer than 10 new foundations in the current fiscal year with the ultimate goal of submitting a winning grant proposal.

Engaging Gift Prospects Is First Step to Setting Visits

Q: **What can we do to get prospects to accept visits from our fundraisers?**

"Try asking them for advice on a specific issue that you know will interest them and bring them back to campus. For example, if your prospect is a former athlete, you could say, 'We're putting together an alumni advisory committee for the promotion of athletics and wanted your advice on how athletics shaped your college experience. We're looking for a few alumni to come back to campus and talk with current students....' If you go into the first meeting asking for advice, you'll get much better results. Make it clear that you are only asking for advice in the first meeting and work in giving after they are engaged. A cold first visit ask is not as successful as a two- to three-visit warm-up ask, even for annual fund gifts. Keep in mind that you're cultivating a lifelong relationship even though you're measured on fiscal year dollars."

— *Sean Devendorf, Director of Annual Giving and Alumni Relations, Friedman School of Nutrition, Tufts University (Boston, MA)*

"When seeking visits with alumni prospects, I have our development officers emphasize that they are seeking to personally connect with people to update them on the university and to explore associations and connections that can benefit a specific college, program or the university in general. I ask each development officer to be an 'honest broker.' That means that if someone they contact is not interested in their college, school or unit, but has a general interest in our university, that they bring that information back so we can reassign the appropriate development officer to be in contact with that person. I also encourage our development officers to use other alums they work with and/or members of their advisory boards to be the primary contact with the prospect and to set up a meeting. People who say they do not want to meet with a development officer are added to a list and a development officer will recontact them a year or two later — if research has found they are good potential prospects — on the premise that their circumstances, mindset, etc. may have changed since we last contacted them."

— *Bruce Mack, Associate Vice President for Development and Alumni Relations, University of Nevada (Reno, NV)*

"I have successfully used two approaches to get visits with prospects — volunteers and focus groups. Use your volunteers (or closer alumni) to help open doors. Many of your alums may be skittish about meeting with you when the call comes from the advancement office when they may be perfectly willing to meet with you and another alum if the call is from the volunteer. Assemble a focus group of alumni representative of those you are looking to visit and ask them how to approach this challenge and why this problem exists. This should provide some very meaningful direct approaches to addressing it."

— *Scott VanDeusen, Executive Director of Advancement Programs, St. John's University (Jamaica, NY)*

Create Prospect Links Where None Appear to Exist

As you peruse other nonprofits' annual reports and walls of honor or read your local paper, you undoubtedly run across names of persons giving to those charities whom you would like to see on your own honor roll of donors.

But how do you go about establishing a relationship with those and other prospects when it appears your organization has no obvious ties?

Here are three ideas for doing just that:

1. **Define the spirit of your mission, then honor a person with those same qualities.** Every state and city has nationally or regionally noted natives who are admired by many. By selecting such a person to be recognized by your organization, you encourage citizens to honor a truly deserving person whose life or activities have helped inspire your own nonprofit to reach higher levels. In doing so, both your organization and your community strengthens positive ties with a respected role model. This may be an annual event honoring a different person each time.

2. **Plan events around historical figures or celebrities who represent your mission or are indigenous to your geographical area.** Make a list of interesting, well-known persons from past or present who can inspire an event or represent a fund drive's theme. Invite the person or his/her descendants to attend, or at least ask for their input on procedures. They may have amusing or inspiring stories to share. This involvement will help make noted and esteemed persons aware of your goals and lead to future involvement.

3. **Join nonconflicting organizations with members you admire.** One of the most effective means for making new contacts is to participate in civic projects that attract motivated or successful individuals. Let those people see your best efforts in action so the admiration becomes mutual and they take interest in you and your work. Even if they are already familiar with your organization, their interest level may be higher knowing capable and caring people like you are involved.

Accept Gifts In-kind to Build Solid Relationships

As you introduce your charity to new contacts and work to strengthen relationships with existing supporters, don't underestimate the value of accepting gifts in-kind. Items, even services, given to your organization can provide the conduit that will eventually lead to major cash gifts — both outright and planned.

Here are two examples that prove how gifts in-kind pave the way for major gifts that follow:

✓ An East Coast hospital accepts artwork on loan, which is prominently displayed in its main lobby along with the owner's name. That ongoing borrowing formula has served as a great introductory point with many persons who, in time, made major cash gifts.

✓ One Midwest college accepted and housed a donor's extensive butterfly collection, a gesture that eventually led to a significant bequest for the institution.

Prospect Involvement Tips

■ Meet with a prospect and ask five questions about his/her perception of your organization. Doing so gives you valuable feedback while involving the prospect in your organization.

Relationship-building Tip

■ It's been said, "When you start relationship building and then stop, it's worse than not having started one." Realize that each new introduction requires ongoing attention and nurturing.

Don't Overlook the Frugal in Pursuit of Major Gifts

Too often, we in the advancement profession tend to look only for persons who generate high incomes as viable gift prospects. What we often fail to do equally as rigorously is identify those who may not be obviously wealthy but are experts at saving and investing their resources.

The lifestyle of many American millionaires is surprisingly frugal. They buy their clothes on sale and off the rack. They drive unassuming vehicles. And on those special occasions when they do choose to dine out, they carefully scrutinize each item on the menu before ordering and on the bill before paying.

The lesson for advancement professionals? Make a concerted effort to pay closer attention to people's saving and spending habits. Your most frugal constituents may, in fact, be among your most viable major gift candidates.

Establish a Long-term Relationship With New Businesses

What do you do when a new business opens in your area? Go beyond sending the token potted plant and be the first nonprofit to bring the owner on board as a supporter.

But rather than running the risk of offending the new businessperson with a premature ask, look for ways to distinguish your organization from the rest by taking steps to establish a positive long-term relationship with the business owner and staff.

Take the following steps to solidify a positive relationship with your community's new businesses:

1. Have employees of your nonprofit on hand for the business' grand opening. Wear name tags or logo clothing that identify the organization you represent.

2. Send a personal welcome letter to the business owner or manager with no strings attached.

3. Host a quarterly breakfast or lunch for community newcomers. Use the occasion to provide a tour of your facilities and offer guests a small memento.

4. If the business executive is new to your community, offer to schedule some time to take him/her around and make introductions to community leaders.

5. Invite the new owner or manager to accompany you as a guest to any civic organizations to which you belong (e.g., Rotary, Sertoma, Optimists Club).

If You See Potential, Keep Pounding Away

Ever come across prospects with both tremendous ability and demonstrated inclination to give, but been unable to align those persons with your organization?

When both of these qualities exist, don't give up.

Many factors affect the consummation of a major gift: timing, approaches, prospect's personal circumstances and more.

As you keep pounding away at various approaches to tell your story, keep an open mind to the possibilities that exist:

- Does it make sense to make contact through the prospect's spouse or another family member?
- Who on your board or in your circle of close friends might help to make an introduction?
- What ties does this prospect have to other businesses, boards or organizations that may provide the needed link?

- Does your organization anticipate a particular event or announcement that could grab this prospect's attention?
- In what ways could you help this prospect experience your organization's worthiness of his/her support?
- What common linkages might exist between this prospect's profession and your organization?
- What strategies might you execute to get this prospect to visit your facility?
- Are there ways to bring your organization's programs or services to this would-be donor?
- As an intermediate step, whom could you attract or what program could you implement that would grab the attention of this probable donor?

Energize Annual Giving Efforts by Engaging Younger Donors

Times are tough in annual giving; participation rates are dropping and donors are giving to fewer organizations. Meanwhile, the number of nonprofits continues to grow.

The key to gaining new annual commitments may be found in younger donors, says Brian Kish, assistant vice president for advancement at Salve Regina University (Newport, RI) and an annual giving consultant with Campbell & Company (Chicago, IL). While older donors already have their loyalties in place, he says, most Generation X and Y donors are free to be courted.

He suggests a three-pronged approach to attracting and sustaining younger donors:

1. **Make it fun.** "Younger generations of donors want to put the fun back in fundraising. It is important to cater to that need. Go ahead and send out the mailers, call them during your phonathon, but when it comes time for the fundraiser, get creative: Throw a party with drinks and music, have a doggie walkathon or a moustache-growing contest. That's how your organization will stand out from the crowd."

2. **Focus on the social.** Where older generations of donors compartmentalized their work, family and civic duties, he says, younger donors are blending their family needs and social needs with philanthropic needs. "This hasn't

been done before," says Kish, "and it means focusing heavily on the social, grassroots aspects of engagement. You want people to be asking one another, 'Are you going to this event? Well then so am I.' This is the most effective way to promote to younger donors."

3. **Early engagement.** The earlier you start engaging potential donors, the better, Kish says. At his institution, most donors making gifts of more than $1,000 have been donating under $1,000 for at least 13 years. Kish says that the likelihood of a donor returning to donate to the same institution increases approximately 20 percent with each year he/she is engaged, so the sooner you start that process, the more support your institution can count on in the long run. At Salve Regina University, fundraisers begin engaging members of the senior class well before graduation. "They may not be able to donate until many years after they've left," Kish says, "but if we engage them while they're still here, when they are able to donate, they will think of us."

Source: Brian Kish, Assistant Vice President for Advancement, Salve Regina University, Newport, RI, and Annual Giving Consultant, Campbell & Company, Chicago, IL. Phone (401) 847-6650. E-mail: annualGiving@campbellcompany.com or brian.kish@salve.edu. Website: www.campbellcompany.com/people/b_kish.html

Cutting Annual Giving Could Undermine Long-term Support

Many organizations are including annual giving programs in budget cuts because, on paper, they earn a lower dollar amount per year, says Brian Kish, assistant vice president for advancement at Salve Regina University (Newport, RI) and an annual giving consultant with Campbell & Company (Chicago, IL). But Kish warns against this strategy, comparing the necessity of annual giving to

research and development in the corporate setting:

"It may seem like the effort of the R&D team is taking a long time to pay off, but when it does, that payoff is huge."

Kish warns that while cutting an annual giving program might save money over the next few years, doing so disables your pipeline of support for the future.

Create a Friend-raising Plan for Pockets of Wealth

Is your nonprofit located close to a resort community of wealthy residents?

Do you have constituents who spend their winters in a wealthy enclave in the South?

Perhaps you're in a major metropolitan area with a suburb of wealthy residents.

Whatever your circumstances, develop a cultivation plan aimed at particular geographic areas where the concentration of wealth is extraordinary. If you can create a presence in such areas, your odds of securing increased major gifts will improve dramatically. Perhaps the competition for philanthropic support will be much greater there, but so too, will your odds for success.

To get started on this important strategy, here's a scenario for establishing visibility in such a pocket of wealth:

1. Identify those wealthy pockets in which you have some existing donors/friends. First identify the pockets of wealth; then determine who (and how many) among your organization's donors/friends reside there. Select the community/area with the greatest potential. (You can add more communities once you have achieved success with your first choice.)

2. Meet with willing individuals to formulate a game plan. Involve donors, board members and others from the designated area in owning your cultivation plan. Review lists of names. Conduct rating/screening sessions. Discuss strategies for gaining visibility.

3. In the beginning, focus on visibility/friend-raising strategies. For example:
   - Ask willing donors to host receptions at varying times throughout the year.
   - Determine ways of bringing your organization to the targeted community. College/university choirs often go on tour and target such key areas, for instance. One Missouri college has a summer theatre located in a resort area. What might your organization have to offer?
   - Provide the area's media with news features about your organization and your connections to that area.
   - Carry out a volunteer project in the area to demonstrate your charity's worthiness.
   - Establish a partnership with a major business in the area and develop a set of mutually beneficial objectives.
   - Establish a satellite office in the community and offer your organization's services in one form or another.

If you have made the decision to focus on major gifts, why not concentrate on those regions that will dramatically improve your odds for success?

Locate and Attract Entrepreneurs to Your Organization

Successful entrepreneurs find a niche in the marketplace that needs to be filled and often make decisions in a short amount of time. Keep this pioneering spirit in mind when approaching an entrepreneur for a major gift, says Lisa M. Dietlin, president and CEO, Lisa M. Dietlin & Associates (Chicago, IL).

So where do you look for entrepreneurs who may be your next major donors?

If your organization is constituent-based, Dietlin says, search your database for titles such as president, CEO, founder or chairman.

If you have no built-in constituency, look for community listings such as the 500 fastest-growing businesses, largest minority-owned businesses, largest women-owned businesses, largest real estate companies, etc. In Dietlin's home base of Chicago, the publication, Crain's Chicago Business, compiles and posts several such lists.

Another place to find entrepreneurs is your local Chamber of Commerce. Tap and cross reference the chamber's list of businesses with your organization's databases for names of persons to contact one on one, and also arrange to make a presentation to all chamber members about the important work your organization does.

On average, entrepreneurs make their first gifts 8.5 years after they start their business, says Dietlin, so keep that in mind when doing this important research.

Source: Lisa M. Dietlin, President & CEO, Lisa M. Dietlin & Associates, Chicago, IL. Phone (773) 772-4465. E-mail: info@lmdietlin.com

Put Out the Welcome Mat

Any time you have the good fortune of bringing someone to your facilities, you have an opportunity to establish and/or strengthen a relationship. That's why it's important to explore every possible opportunity to bring people to your organization and provide them with a positive experience.

Evaluate Procedures for Guests Who Pay a Visit

What's your procedure for handling expected or unexpected guests who visit your offices?

As often as we in advancement take our organizations out to donors and would-be donors, it's easy to take walk-ins and scheduled guests for granted. Yet there is no better opportunity to cultivate a relationship than when a person is willing to take time to visit you on your own turf.

In addition to providing an inviting and friendly reception area with readily available literature about your organization, here are some hospitality pointers to help your guests feel more welcome:

Scheduled Guests —

- Inform the receptionist of scheduled appointments so guests can be greeted by name: "Good morning, Mrs. Lancaster. Todd is expecting you."
- If the individual is an infrequent visitor, ask him/her to sign your guest book.
- Have a photograph of the guest taken with someone and sent as a memento.
- Offer to provide a personal tour of your facilities with you as the guide.
- When appropriate, introduce guest(s) to other employees, especially your CEO.

Unscheduled Walk-ins —

- If you are out of the office and a visitor prefers to meet

Five Ways to Maximize Guest Visits

When you're fortunate enough to have donors and potential donors come to you:

1. Allow them to see your organization in action, observing those being served.
2. Take note of stops along your tour that pique guests' interests. These may provide funding clues.
3. Allow others in the development department to meet and greet the visitor.
4. Stop by the CEO's office for a brief "hello."
5. Point out key physical plant features: anticipated capital improvements, new state-of-the-art equipment, etc.

---

with you, instruct your assistant to schedule a return visit or an appointment at a location of the guest's choice.
- Instruct the receptionist to bring in a capable substitute if you are unavailable.
- Have trained staff on call to provide facility tours at a moment's notice.

Develop a standard follow-up letter and brief survey that invites guests to share impressions of their recent visit. The impression your guests receive will clearly impact their enthusiasm to invest in your cause.

Use Construction Period to Cultivate Prospects, Donors

If you are in the midst of a construction or renovation project and aren't inviting donors and would-be donors to witness the process, you're missing a great cultivation opportunity.

For most nonprofits, a major construction/renovation is an infrequent occurrence. And when it does take place — even if somewhat messy — most people will perceive the changes being made as progress. The noise, the construction workers, the chaos surrounding the project are all perceived as steps toward an enhanced environment.

To get the most from your organization's construction project:

1. Invite small groups of donors and would-be donors to view the project at various points in the construction phase. Think about whether it's to your advantage to mix donors with prospects or target each group sepa-

rately. Both have their advantages.
2. Pay attention to detail and safety issues. For instance, you may wish to use golf carts for a large-scale tour or distribute hard hats in an active construction zone.
3. Have persons on hand who can point out changes taking place and how those changes will impact those served by your organization.
4. Conclude the tour with refreshments and brief remarks by your CEO or board chair, thanking those who have invested in the project and inviting those who have not to give serious thought to their level of support.

Following your construction or renovation tour, make it standard practice to follow up in setting appointments with attendees who have yet to make a pledge.

Tours Get Major Donors Passionate About Your Cause

In February 2009, development staff with The Clinic (Phoenixville, PA), a medical clinic for the uninsured, began offering donor prospects tours to get them engaged and passionate about supporting the clinic's mission.

The 30-minute clinic tours are conducted near the end of business day, between 3:30 and 4 p.m., and led by Debbie Shupp, development director, or Krys Sipple, the clinic's executive director.

> *"Involvement in the tours makes our board members feel good... They are not expected to ask for money, just to tell their story."*

Tours end in Sipple's office, with the opportunity for the participants to chat with a board member and ask questions.

"Involvement in the tours makes our board members feel good," says Shupp. "I've never had a board member say they won't do it. They are not expected to ask for money, just to tell their story."

About 60 percent of the board has participated in the tours, and the rest haven't only because they haven't had an opportunity yet, she says, "We've only held about two dozen tours so far."

At the end of each tour, participants are given brochures, newsletters and sometimes event invitations, thanked and invited to come back.

Shupp recruits tour participants when networking at organizations, churches, clubs and the Chamber of Commerce. "I always give out my card and ask if they are interested in coming in for a tour," she says.

She also recruits tour participants by tracking consistent donors. "I do this by looking at gifts that reflect the donor's care for the clinic," she says. "I call them to thank them for their gift and ask if they've been here. If not, I ask them to come in for a tour."

Once someone is brought in for a tour, he or she is always on board, says Shupp: "We've had donors say 'You painted the walls!' or 'Wow, I didn't expect you to have done this or that.' When they do, I always ask, 'What were you expecting?' The donor might say, 'Cold, cement walls.' And I will reply, 'We have great volunteers here who have worked to paint all the rooms and keep everything nice.'"

Shupp follows up after the tour with an e-mail thank you. She also adds the tour participants to the clinic's mailing list.

The tours have been very successful in attracting donors, she says: "Seventy-five percent of those who go on the tours end up making a donation. Donations range from $50 to several thousand dollars."

In addition to attracting donations, the tours have also been great at building relationships, says Shupp. For example, she says, one tour participant from a local church asked to be an outreach partner for the clinic, and another asked to help with the clinic's wish list.

Source: Debbie Shupp, Development Director, The Clinic, Phoenixville, PA. Phone (610) 935-1134, ext. 24. E-mail: dshupp@theclinicpa.org

Make Groundbreaking Magic

Breaking ground for a major facility or renovation is the opportune time to celebrate donors, generate new gifts and boost awareness of your capital campaign. To generate the highest level of community participation and media recognition:

- **Start with the architect's rendering.** Use the drawing in press releases and in a fundraising brochure that includes facts about how the building will enhance services, plus a pledge envelope.

- **Ask supporters and employees to fill a time capsule.** Make your groundbreaking memorable by burying a time capsule of items significant to your mission and history. Have attendees sign a banner to put inside.

- **Invite a well-known local or regional celebrity.** Ideally, that person will have some interest in your mission and be able to make brief remarks. Present him/her with a decorated honorary shovel or hard hat as a souvenir, and take plenty of photos for press releases or publications.

- **Pour a cement slab.** Then let your board members, employees and supporters leave a thumbprint, initials, a colorful stone or other memento set into the cement.

- **Hold an outdoor picnic.** Have a large tent, refreshments, games, speeches and even a contest for a facility name if one hasn't been chosen. Offer toy shovels to let children break ground themselves. The photo opportunities alone are priceless, and can be used in ongoing fundraising literature.

Get the Most Mileage Out of Donor Photos

When donors visit your facilities to attend a reception, see a project or program they helped fund or meet with recipients of their generosity, chances are you or your staff may take photos of the donors on site. What do you do next? Do you simply store the photos on your hard drive or in a file cabinet, never to be seen again?

Here are some options for making the best use of donor photos:

✓ Send a photo of the donor to the donor along with a personal note of gratitude.

✓ If the donor's gift helped a specific person (e.g., scholarship recipient, patient), send that person a photo with a note saying, "Perhaps you will be able to assist someone one day just as this person assisted you."

✓ Keep a photo in the donor's file so staff can identify donors when they visit again.

✓ Develop a feature story to accompany each photo that can be pitched to the media. Maintain an up-to-date file of feature possibilities.

✓ Maintain a yearly photo album in your lobby or a wall display that depicts your nonprofit's ties to its many donors.

Keep Open House Relevant

The open house can be the most effective and efficient way to raise awareness about your mission. Highly successful open houses have one thing in common — they stay on message. To assure your open house accomplishes what it should:

❑ **Show your good works.** Beyond showing off your facility, an open house is an invaluable opportunity to advertise your organization's accomplishments. Think of your physical space as a map to guide a sight-seeing tour of achievements; set up stations for visitors to learn more about what you do, how you do it, and how successful you have been. Include special guests who can attest to your success, such as experts in your field, or beneficiaries of your organization's work.

❑ **Put a (pleasant) face to the name.** Your organization can be doing all the good work in the world, but without physical symbols to attach it to, that work may not translate. Use your open house to present a symbol to attach value to: This could be a leader or beneficiary in your organization or a take-away item such as a button or ribbon that helps solidify your organization's symbolism in donors' minds.

❑ **Connect to your donor pool.** The open house is not only a meet-and-greet from the donor's perspective, but also from yours. Include time for your staff to ask donors why they are attending the open house to engage them on a more personal, specific level. Have staff discreetly take notes so you can recall what initially attracted the donor to your organization.

❑ **Get specific about fundraising needs.** Don't be afraid to talk about very specific needs while on the tour; your financial needs will translate all the more when you speak about them in context. You never know when a specific need may fit perfectly with a donor's experience or ability to give.

❑ **Make it your own.** Find spaces, stations, guests and take-aways that are unique to your organization. With the right touch, your open houses can garner a reputation for being a must-attend event within your community. Your open house should be a fundraiser in your mind, but a "fun"raiser in the minds of your guests.

Prospect Cultivation Idea

Ever thought about partnering with a local manufacturer, retailer or other business to provide sample products as gifts for out-of-town prospects with whom you meet? This is a great way to involve the business in addition to getting donated gifts.

Courting the Wealthy, Second Edition.
Edited by Scott C. Stevenson.
© 2010 Stevenson, Inc. Published 2010 by Stevenson, Inc.

Relationship building can take on many forms and be directed to various groups and individuals based on any number of factors: age, gender, affiliation with your organization, geographic location, financial capability and more. Targeting your cultivation to particular groups allows you to make the relationship-building experience more personal and meaningful and is much more cost-effective than attempting to be all things to all people.

Target Particular Groups With Involvement Opportunities

Want to generate more and increased gifts? Work at increasing involvement among both donors and would-be donors. As you know, involvement leads to investment.

To improve the level of involvement, however, strive to offer opportunities matching the interests of particular groups. For example, the volunteer projects you suggest to former board members may be different than those you would offer young professionals or recent high school graduates.

Examples of segmentation may include:

- Alumni
- Specific professions
- Singles
- Young families
- Retired employees
- Women/men
- New graduates
- Scout or 4-H groups
- Community service opportunities
- Families of those you serve
- Baby boomers
- Parents
- Businesses
- Civic organizations
- Senior citizens
- Former board members
- Environmental activists
- Church groups

Elkhorn Council
on Sexual Assault & Domestic Violence

Involvement Opportunities for Former Board Members...

Name _____
Address _____
City/State/ZIP _____
Phone _____ E-mail _____

❑ Mentor a new board member ❑ Help identify awards recipients
❑ Host a reception ❑ Help host appreciation banquet
❑ Conduct stewardship calls ❑ Conduct VIP tours
❑ Screen prospect names ❑ Help make new introductions
❑ Make business contacts ❑ Other_____

This is an example of an inquiry card that could be used to encourage former board members to renew their involvement with a nonprofit.

After identifying targeted groups, develop involvement opportunity menus aimed at their interests and/or skills. Then market those opportunities through one-on-one visits, direct mail, online, group presentations and more.

Steps Help Cultivate Donors Who Live Far Away

Often, a nonprofit has a contingent of donors who keep the cause close in their hearts even though they may be far removed from it geographically.

How do you cultivate relationships and maintain interest with these important planned gift prospects and donors who live far from your organization: alumni, former residents of your community, chapter members and others?

To cultivate and steward long-distance supporters you may not be able to visit as often as you would prefer:

✓ **Establish a tickler system.** Send regular messages from your institution at irregular intervals. Create a monthly reminder of who should receive a phone call, birthday or anniversary card or other appropriate (but not contrived) communications.

✓ **Provide a virtual tour.** Besides offering a virtual tour of your facilities on your website, annually produce a video that can be distributed to all geographically distant prospects. Include a narrated tour of your facility and interviews with employees and those you serve. For older prospects, produce a nostalgic I remember when documentary.

✓ **Send there's-no-place-like-home reminders.** For former area residents, mail products or e-mail links of hometown flavor, from products produced in your region to books/periodicals with regional flavor or news clippings from your local newspaper.

✓ **Include personal notes with each planned gifts newsletter.** If you produce a quarterly planned gifts newsletter, include an occasional personal note for some of your far-away clients to personalize the mailing.

Although scheduling visits to viable planned gift prospects at least once a year is advantageous, these cultivation strategies will serve to strengthen ties with these key individuals.

Target Under-40 Audience

To cultivate successive generations of leadership, the Dallas Museum of Art (Dallas, TX) offers the Junior Associates Circle. For persons under age 40, the circle offers many of the full $2,000 associate membership benefits for $625 a year, says Kimberly Bryan, director of donor circle membership.

One challenge of targeting younger supporters, Bryan says, is that they tend to be highly transient, and relationships can be lost when people relocate. But, she notes, outweighing that are the benefits of engaging people at a young age in a relationship that can last decades.

To attract and keep a young audience, Bryan recommends strong volunteer leadership that nurtures peer-to-peer interaction.

Source: Kimberly Camuel Bryan, Director of Donor Circle Membership, Dallas Museum of Art, Dallas, TX. Phone (214) 922-1242. E-mail: kbryan@DallasMuseumofArt.org

Connect With Your Community's Native Sons and Daughters

Based on the type of nonprofit you represent — your mission, programs and services — could you justify a program intended to connect with former residents of your community — people who were born or grew up there but now live elsewhere?

Find a sincere way to connect with native sons and daughters and there's no limit on what you can do to cultivate relationships with financially capable individuals who are part of this group.

Here are some examples of how you might cultivate relationships with your city's or state's natives:

1. **Start a Who's Who of your city or service region.** Work at building a list of natives who have gone on to achieve success and any degree of celebrity. This becomes your working list of those to be approached and cultivated. Talk to old-timers who can help identify those persons. Visit with the alumni offices of your city's colleges, universities and schools to identify their Who's Who lists. Talk to chamber of commerce officials to see if such a list already exists in their office. You may even decide to form a Who's Who advisory committee to help with this undertaking.

2. **Identify ways to reconnect natives with their hometown (or state).** Share news clippings, historical accounts and more. Involve old friends and relatives to help re-establish ties and make introductions with your organization.

3. **Take the lead in establishing a yearly event that invites former residents back.** If a community festival of some sort already exists, use that as a homecoming connecting point.

4. **Initiate an annual awards program that selects community natives based on their achievements.** You may choose to collaborate with your local chamber or other organizations to make this program more encompassing.

5. **Build a Web page geared to your community's native sons and daughters.** Share your who's who list on the site and include brief biographies on each or limit them to past awards recipients. Include links to your community's history and points of interest. Offer trivia questions about your community to which visitors can respond. Include a gallery of former residents' photos.

Work Geographic Pockets of Wealth

If generating increased numbers of major gifts is your goal, make time to conceptualize what can be done to target the wealthy in geographically concentrated areas.

Examples might include:

- Selecting specific ZIP codes in your community or service area and conducting particular direct mail efforts.
- Regularly visiting and networking locations throughout the nation that have higher concentrations of wealthy constituents.

- Coordinating get-acquainted receptions of any sort in wealthy neighborhoods throughout your community or region.

- Convincing an existing board member or donor to purchase a gift membership for your CEO to exclusive clubs where he/she can rub shoulders with persons of means.

Symphony Reaches Out to Physicians

Look for ways to bring together like-minded individuals for the benefit of your cause.

The Physicians for the Phoenix Symphony was formed 22 years ago by a group of symphony patrons from the medical community who wanted to take a leadership role in recognizing The Phoenix Symphony (Phoenix, AZ) as an important cultural resource.

"The group continues to sponsor concerts, hold fundraising events and private recitals, and share their enjoyment of symphonic music," says Frank E. Bourget, director of development.

The 60-member volunteer group, led by a chair and a six- to eight-person executive committee, meets monthly to discuss recruitment strategies and plan events. Members are recruited through personal contact, networking, the symphony website and event publicity.

Members' dues range from $50 to $1,500 annually, and several members give additional annual fund gifts of $10,000.

"The Physicians for the Phoenix Symphony has helped in the cultivation of major gifts by introducing us to new major gift prospects who became more involved with the symphony by attending our events, and attending more concerts and becoming new annual donors and season series subscribers," says Bourget. One member, he notes, even secured a $25,000 gift from the corporation he worked for to sponsor a concert.

Members of the group organized several cultivation events in October and November 2008, including a pre-concert reception and a recital at a private home. A private concert at Steinway of Phoenix, and a salon concert at a private home, raised $5,000 each.

"Gifts usually result after further contact by major gifts staff, who make follow-up calls or send notes to people they engaged with at the event," says Bourget.

Source: Frank E. Bourget, Director of Development, The Phoenix Symphony, Phoenix, AZ. Phone (602) 452-0420. E-mail: fbourget@phoenixsymphony.org

Three Tips for Winning Over a Reluctant Spouse

So you have the gift in sight that will take your organization to the next level. There's just one problem — the reluctant spouse. Your donor is ready to write the check, but his/her spouse isn't convinced.

Lisa Grove, deputy director and director of development, Contemporary Art Museum St. Louis (St. Louis, MO), says that challenge isn't insurmountable. Using these tips may help you get the gift:

- **Meet with the spouse one-on-one.** As long as you get the go-ahead from the donor, this can open a fresh avenue of communication. The spouse may be more comfortable discussing reasons behind his/her reluctance if the donor is not present. This meeting can also help you to build a relationship directly with this person who has such influence on your major donor prospect.

- **Structure the gift in recognition of the donor.** Consider using the gift as a naming opportunity to honor the donor's support of your organization. The spouse may appreciate the effort you're making in recognizing the donor's hard work on your behalf.

- **Give the donor and his/her spouse some control.** Let them jointly make some decisions about how the gift will be used.

Once you secure the gift, make sure to thank the spouse individually for helping to make it happen.

Source: Lisa Grove, Deputy Director and Director of Development, Contemporary Art Museum St. Louis, St. Louis, MO. Phone (314) 535-4660. E-mail: lgrove@camstl.org

Engage Young Donors

Q: What is one challenge you've overcome in working with young donors?

"Our challenge was developing a hands-on, exclusive opportunity that would engage the group and respect the age range — parents with young families won't be reached with a happy hour. Instead, we offered a program opportunity to 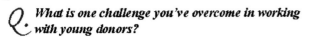 the Young Leaders for Medicine previously available only to our senior community leaders — and that was the ticket! Our Leadership Grand Rounds program is a unique opportunity for 15 to 20 committed young leaders at a time to spend a half day at the hospital with a host group of leading physicians. This hands-on doctor-for-a-day experience engages the group two-fold: Instant information is exchanged to equip these advocates with messaging for their community peers and mentors; and it provides time for exclusive fellowship in an intimate group setting."

Source: Erin Meade, Development Officer, The Methodist Hospital Group, Houston, TX. Phone (832) 667-5806. E-mail: Emeade@tmhs.org

Committee Empowers Donors

Donors are unique in the ways they give and in what motivates them to give.

One Iowa foundation has found a way to celebrate the distinct giving trends of one group of donors while reaping the benefits.

For nine years, the Iowa State University (ISU) Foundation (Ames, IA) has invited female donors to serve on its women and philanthropy committee and act as advocates for ISU and for philanthropy.

Women chosen to serve are interested in philanthropy and interested in empowering women, says Melissa Hanna, executive director of annual and special giving.

The committee hosts an annual women and philanthropy workshop where, through keynote speakers and breakout sessions, women learn about creating and maintaining healthy financial positions.

"The committee definitely brings women to the forefront," Hanna says. "We want to focus more attention on that constituency and make sure their philanthropic needs are met. We want women to feel empowered and know they have a voice in this discussion as well."

The proof of the committee's efforts is in the numbers. According to Hanna:

✓ The foundation experienced a 47 percent increase in total number of women donors since 2000. The number jumped from 72,095 women donors by Dec. 31, 2000, to 105,816 by Dec. 31, 2008.

✓ The average gift from a woman increased 184 percent from $597 in FY 2003 to $1,696 in FY 2008.

✓ Through 2008, women have given more than $218 million to ISU.

The women and philanthropy committee comprises 17 women from varying professions, all with an interest in ISU. Members may serve two, two-year terms, with those holding the position of board chair granted an extra term. The committee typically meets five times a school year with the first meeting being a fall retreat.

Source: Melissa Hanna, Executive Director of Annual and Special Giving, Iowa State University Foundation, Ames, IA. Phone (515) 294-0596. E-mail: mhanna@foundation.iastate.edu

Founding the Philanthropic Women of St. Joseph's

With generous gifts of $25,000 each, Donna Jordan and Elaine F. Shimberg founded Philanthropic Women of St. Joseph's (PWSJ), a giving group that supports St. Joseph's Hospital Foundation (Tampa, FL).

The founders receive permanent recognition as Philanthropic Women and are permanent members of the group's steering committee. Their gifts are pooled with other members' and together the entire membership chooses a funding project to support each year.

"After becoming a foundation board member, I was presented with the most exciting challenge of all: Philanthropic Women of St. Joseph's Hospital," says Jordan.

"This endeavor had not been done with any hospital in our area; we would be the first. Also, it was an opportunity to work with my mentor, Elaine Shimberg," she says. "Through the PWSJ, my commitment has become stronger than ever. It has given me an opportunity to bring in friends, old and new, and to introduce them to and educate them about the mission of St. Joseph's Hospital. We have had opportunities to meet doctors, nurses and administrative staff and learn the latest in cutting-edge technology as well as specific needs of the hospital."

Jordan says the philanthropic group also allows them "to bring in talented women in our area who otherwise might not have been involved in the hospital unless they were faced with a specific health need. These women we bring in will, in turn, bring their friends and acquaintances into the St. Joseph's family. This will enable us to expand and multiply

our talents and potential funding. Each year we will then see how our specific gifts have impacted the women and children of our community. It's been an exciting and fulfilling time."

Shimberg has served as volunteer at St. Joseph's Hospitals for more than 25 years, serving on several hospital committees and as chair of the hospital's board of trustees. She currently serves as chair of the St. Joseph's Hospital Foundation Board.

"I loved the idea of Philanthropic Women of St. Joseph's because it was a way to bring in new faces and helping hands," Shimberg says. "I knew that the more our community's young women knew about St. Joseph's Hospital, the more they'd want to continue their involvement and enjoy supporting it financially. Having Donna Jordan as a co-founder has infused the group with an amazing energy and enthusiasm.

"It has strengthened my commitment to the hospital because it reminds me of why I got involved so many years ago — the high quality and compassion of those working in the hospital, the enthusiasm of those volunteers I grew to know as friends as we created fundraisers, community promotions, etc. Lastly, I must admit, the energy of our PWSJ members has recharged my batteries as well. It's fun!"

Sources: Donna Jordan, Founder, and Elaine F. Shimberg, Founder, Philanthropic Women of St. Joseph's, St. Joseph's Hospital Foundation, Tampa, FL. Phone (813) 872-0979. E-mail: sjhfoundation@baycare.org

When Developing Donor Relationships, Don't Overlook Other Nonprofits

When considering potential donors, many fundraisers get stuck in the mindset that only major business entities will be in a position to give to their cause.

Such an approach may be shortsighted.

Keep in mind that giving is a major part of the mission of many clubs, faith-based organizations and other not-for-profit groups of all sizes. So it makes sense to consider them as viable donors to your cause.

So how does one go about soliciting a nonprofit organization? In many ways, the process is no different than soliciting a business or individual: the key is in developing meaningful relationships that result in a mutual benefit, says Carol Kline, executive director of development and the Jefferson College Foundation (Hillsboro, MO).

"It's about finding the kinds of places that have a similar goal," says Kline, whose school recently entered into a scholarship agreement with her local chapter of the Philanthropic Education Organization (PEO-FR). In the agreement,

PEO-FR sponsors an annual scholarship at the Jefferson College, and in exchange, the Jefferson College Foundation maintains the scholarship on the administrative end. "This makes it easier on them," says Kline, "and we know that we can count on them for that gift every year. Everyone benefits, and it is a commitment we will share forever."

Kline calls this sort of mutually beneficial work friend-raising; the only difference between nonprofit donor cultivation and business cultivation, she says, is that both parties in a nonprofit-to-nonprofit relationship already speak the language of the fundraiser. So rather than years of wining and dining, there are years of working closely together on projects in which both parties are already invested. Eventually, the philanthropic relationship blossoms naturally.

Source: Carol Kline, Executive Director of Development and the Jefferson College Foundation, Jefferson College, Hillsboro, MO. Phone (636) 797-3000. E-mail: ckline1@jeffco.edu. Website: www.jeffco.edu

Create Programs Aimed at Building Relationships

There are any number of strategies you can use to create and solidify relationships with would-be donors: clubs and societies with accompanying benefits, awards, affinity groups, mailings, group travel and more. This chapter offers a sampling of programs and strategies you can use toward that end.

Travel Programs Can Enhance Fundraising Efforts

Consider offering opportunities for your major donors to mix and mingle, for both short and extended periods, to nurture their connections to your organization and one another.

One way to do so is to offer travel opportunities. Judge interest levels and build camaraderie among this important group with day-long jaunts to choice destinations within your service region. If those prove successful, move to one- or two-night stays that include destinations and adventures that appeal to your major supporters.

Next step? A travel program that offers the opportunity to travel to desirable destinations across the country and planet.

Here, two organizations share information about their travel programs — the first of which offers travel to major donors as well as other supporters of its organization, and the second which offers travel as a benefit exclusively to major donors:

McGill University (Montreal, Quebec, Canada):

Each year, McGill University (Montreal, Quebec, Canada) offers 25 to 30 educational travel opportunities for interested alumni, parents and friends. Destinations include Antarctica, Egypt, Peru, Japan and Nepal.

"At McGill we have not looked at the travel program as a breeding ground for major gifts," says Leisha LeCouvie, director of parent and affinity programs. "That being said, some of our travelers have been very generous. There is no formal major gift solicitation process in place, but rather we depend on our hosts to bring home information that may lead to intense cultivation."

Although the travel program does not directly increase major gifts, LeCouvie says there is an indirect benefit because of the engagement.

"A trip host is an excellent ambassador for the university and is able to speak about areas of need, interesting new research and current students," she says. "Our travelers generally are of an age that affords them luxuries, such as the trips, and more freedom to even consider larger annual fund or major gifts."

Approximately 350 people participate in the travel program each year.

After the trip, the host shares any information that may indicate participants' proclivity to give with university fundraisers, who in turn determine whether to call on the prospect.

The Museum of Contemporary Art (MOCA) of Los Angeles, CA:

The travel program at MOCA is offered as a member benefit, with 40 to 50 people traveling to places like New York, Chicago, China, Germany and India each year.

"Our program is above all a donor benefit," says Veridiana Pontes-Ring, donor programs manager. "Our trips are exclusive and focus on giving participants the most exclusive VIP opportunities available and the best in contemporary art, design, hotel experience and cuisine."

Eligibility for local outings and day trips is for members contributing at the $650 level. Trips within the United States and to art fairs are for those contributing $1,500 and $4,500, while international trips are typically reserved for partners at the $10,000 level and trustees.

"MOCA travel is an important cultivation tool for the museum, providing an opportunity to spend time with our patrons and donors outside the museum and office in a unique art environment," Pontes-Ring says. "It has also proven to be an important benefit when members consider upgrading to MOCA Partner membership ($10,000)." Additionally, she says, "The travel program gives members the sense of community and makes them feel an active part of the museum. Members learn from higher-level donors and trustees, become friends and become active members of the MOCA community."

All members and visitors to the art museum benefit indirectly from the trips, says Pontes-Ring, as the ventures often lead to donations of artwork as well as donations to support exhibitions.

Sources: Leisha LeCouvie, Director of Parent and Affinity Programs, McGill University, Alumni Services, Montreal, Quebec, Canada. Phone (514) 398-1578. E-mail: leisha.lecouvie@mcgill.ca Veridiana Pontes-Ring, The Museum of Contemporary Art, Los Angeles, CA. Phone (213) 621-1778. E-mail: mocatravel@moca.org

Anniversary Lends Itself to Celebrating, Wooing Major Donors

When staff and supporters of the University of Southern California Thornton School of Music (Los Angeles, CA) began planning for its 125th anniversary two years ago, they began to think of every conceivable way to capitalize on the anniversary — and the number 125 — to attract gifts.

"Our message was that it may be our 125th anniversary, but that this was about building the next 125 years, and that takes resources," says Robert Cutietta, dean. "We

> *"We planned a lot of high-profile events for people who give, which has provided many opportunities to showcase our donors."*

decided early on to get everyone on board with our message being about building our future. We weren't ashamed that our future included a need for money."

They planned concerts with 125 in the opus. They designed gifts with 125 in them, soliciting a $1.25 million gift, eight $125,000 gifts, and encouraging alums to increase their $100 gifts to $125 in the spirit of the school's 125th anniversary. Over the course of the 125 days of celebration (Aug. 9-Dec. 11, 2009), the university hosted lectures, concerts or some type of event literally every day, says Cutietta.

"We planned a lot of high-profile events for people who give, which has provided many opportunities to showcase our donors," he says. "The campaign has been very successful and a lot of fun. Everyone has gotten into it."

Thirty-one days into the 125 days of celebration, the school held a celebratory dinner and concert that attracted 700 alumni and donors. "We wanted to hold our first large event fairly early into the celebration to show donors the kind of publicity the campaign would get," says Cutietta. Each gift was announced individually, followed by a two to three minute performance tied to the gift, e.g., if the gift was made to the piano program, a student played a short piano piece.

"Donors loved it," he says. "The event attracted more interest from prospective donors. Alums who hadn't been back for years made gifts of $1,250 instead of the $125 gifts we had asked for because they were inspired by the 125th anniversary."

As of Oct. 15, nearly halfway into the 125-day celebration, organizers had raised $2.5 million, all from gifts that had the number 125 in them or were multiples of 125. Two of those gifts were matching gifts and were used to encourage additional $125 gifts, says Cutietta.

The celebration concluded with an anniversary formal gala dinner. Donors who wished to be acknowledged at the Dec. 11 event had to make their gift by that date.

The cultivation and solicitation of major donors has been done almost exclusively in person. No written proposals were used. "My wife and I invited one or two couples to dinner, and small groups of donors were invited to a special dinner before certain events," he says.

Alums have received three mailings over nine months. The first alerted them of the 125th anniversary celebrations. The second announced the launch of the celebration and invited them to return to campus for anniversary-related events. Neither of the first two mailings included a solicitation. The third mailing included a specific ask.

No printed material was produced specifically for the campaign. Instead, 125th anniversary logos were added to existing materials. School officials created gifts instead, including crystal glasses and computer jump drives with the 125th anniversary logo.

The 125 days of celebration provided numerous opportunities for media coverage, including a full-page spread in the LA Times, as well as articles in targeted music publications. "We did very focused announcements about different programs at the school that would be attractive to specific publications," Cutietta says. "For example, we talked about jazz gifts to the jazz world and piano gifts to the piano world."

The keys to their success were starting really early with the planning and deciding early on what their message would be, says Cutietta: "Our focused, simple message really captivated people. We also got everyone on board internally first and hired an outside firm to help keep us focused. It helped to have an outsider who doesn't know anything about the internal politics and limitations involved."

Source: Robert Cutietta, Dean, USC Thornton School of Music, Los Angeles, CA. Phone (213) 740-5389.
E-mail: MusicDean@Thornton.usc.edu

Create Programs Aimed at Building Relationships

Draw More Major Donors With Upper-level Membership Perks

How does an organization ensure that upper-level memberships ($1,000 per year and up) are attractive to individuals of means? By providing at least one of three things, says Lauren Davidson, individual giving manager at the Contemporary Jewish Museum (CJM) of San Francisco, CA: access, recognition or opportunities for socialization.

Museum benefits offering access include priority admission, curator-led tours and invitations to exclusive receptions and artist events. Recognition-based benefits include an annual donor wall, newsletter mention and the option to underwrite major exhibitions and programs.

In offering upper-level benefits, Davidson says, they take into consideration that high-end donors may see the value of benefits differently than persons who give at lesser levels. Davidson takes recognition as an example, noting that the desire for public acknowledgement often wanes at the highest levels of giving.

"People giving $10,000 to one institution are often giving it to several others," she says, "so recognition is not as important to them. We find it generally matters more to those in the $1,000 to $5,000 range because many of them give only to us."

Similarly, Davidson says, when offering social opportunities, museum officials often distinguish between on-site events (generally offered at the $1,000 level) and off-site events (offered at $1,800 and up). Doing so, she says, provides a gradation of benefits that encourages individuals to upgrade memberships.

Regarding value benefits such as guest passes and gift shop discounts, she says that when it comes to upper-level donors, "these are not hugely compelling, but they're not meaningless, either," noting that members at the $1,000-plus levels do make use of discounts and special sales.

The most important step to determining benefits that both reward members and encourage them to move up giving levels, she says, is understanding members' fundamental motivation. "We find about 75 percent of higher-level donors are mission-based, rather than benefits-based. The key, then, is structuring benefits to make sure those individuals feel involved with the institution they believe in. It all comes back to building and strengthening relationships."

Source: Lauren Davidson, Individual Giving Manager, Contemporary Jewish Museum, San Francisco, CA. Phone (415) 655-7829. E-mail: Ldavidson@thecjm.org

Annual Giving Societies Attract $1,000-plus Donors

Give donors the opportunity to support your cause in ways that let them network, socialize and have fun, and you'll greatly increase the likelihood they will continue supporting you for the long run.

Children's Healthcare of Atlanta (Atlanta, GA), for example, has two annual leadership giving societies for $1,000-plus donors: Hope's Circle for female donors and Will's Club for male donors.

Hope's Circle, started five years ago, has nearly 250 members. Will's Club, started about a year ago with about 25 donors, has nearly tripled in size to almost 70 members.

Both are opt-in, meaning members are not automatically enrolled, but must agree to join, says Elesha Mavrommatis, development officer. "The opt-in feature helps us identify donors who want to be contacted on a regular basis," she says. "In effect, they self-identify as being open to a call from a development officer."

Hope's Circle members receive a monthly e-newsletter as well as invitations to behind-the-scenes tours, roundtable discussions with physicians, luncheons and other donor events. Will's Club members receive a quarterly e-newsletter and invitations to member-hosted events. Both groups are recognized in the organization's community report, on signage at the hospitals, and on the medical facility's website.

"While Hope's Circle is staff-driven — I coordinate tours and events — Will's Club is member-driven," says Mavrommatis. "Will's Club members plan their own events and are more active recruiters for the group. For the men, it's

a way to socialize with other men who want to support the hospital. I believe that long-term, the men's group will be successful because they feel ownership of it."

Events organized by the men's group to date include skeet shooting, a wine tasting, a tour and tasting at a local brewery.

Mavrommatis says switching giving society membership due dates from anniversary date to calendar year has made tracking membership much easier. For example, members who give in 2009 are recognized as 2009 donors and have all of 2010 to make a qualifying gift for the next fiscal year.

When a qualifying gift comes in through the annual fund, staff send an acknowledgement that includes the opportunity to join the giving society and how to do so.

"When we call them to thank them for their gift, we will also mention it again," she says. "Once they join Hope's Circle, we call to welcome them and send them the last e-newsletter that went out, which includes my contact information sent under my e-mail address. This helps me develop a relationship with these donors."

Will's Club communicates almost exclusively through e-mail.

At Thanksgiving, Mavrommatis sends handwritten cards to both society members which she says helps develop a relationship with these donors, which is an important element in the success of the giving societies.

Source: Elesha Mavrommatis, Development Officer, Children's Healthcare of Atlanta, Atlanta, GA. Phone (404) 785-7336. E-mail: Elesha.Mavrommatis@choa.org

Create Programs Aimed at Building Relationships

Heritage Circle Giving Society Focuses on $1,000-plus Donors

Staff with the Wisconsin Historical Foundation (Madison, WI) — the official fundraising and gift-receiving organization for the Wisconsin History Society — are focusing on increasing members of its $1,000-plus-a-year Heritage Circle level.

"We've added benefits for members at this level including invitations to exclusive events and activities, complimentary gift VIP parking privileges, and special recognition in our Honor Roll of Donors and Members in addition to the regular benefits of society membership," says Jeanne L. Engle, the foundation's director of development.

Between July 1, 2009, (the start of the Wisconsin Historical Foundation's fiscal year) and Jan. 5, 2010, some 64 donors had made commitments for unrestricted gifts of $1,000 or more, qualifying them for membership in The Heritage Circle. This was up from 49 such donors during the same time in the previous fiscal year, says Martha Truby, associate director of annual giving.

Organizers developed a special package for soliciting prospective members from The Heritage Circle level that includes:

- A letter inviting prospective donors to join The Heritage Circle (to which a development staff member or officer usually add a handwritten note).

- A Heritage Circle brochure — a tri-fold with a pocket into which a list of Heritage Circle donors and a list of Heritage Circle benefits is inserted.

- A customized reply device.

"As we qualify donors who have been identified with having higher financial capacity, we make a personal appeal for membership in The Heritage Circle," says Engle. These personal appeals may be a letter with a handwritten note, a face-to-face visit or a phone call.

To build awareness for The Heritage Circle, they branded it separately with a special logo embedded with the tag line: Leading the Way.

"We created a separate logo because we wanted to reinforce the message that membership in the Heritage Circle means being part of something special," says Truby. "Our goal is to engage them with small group cultivation events, behind-the-scenes tours and insider information. Savvy investors are passionate about our mission and we want them to understand the impact they have on our organization by offering them opportunities to become engaged in what we do."

One new benefit is allowing members to choose their own complimentary gift, says Truby. They can choose one of four books produced by the Wisconsin Historical Society Press, or one of four prints reproduced from the society's extensive image collection. "This is offered with a coupon that is sent with their Heritage Circle member packet," she says. "Several recipients of the coupon added a thank-you note saying they really appreciated the gift."

A key to their early success in attracting Heritage Circle members has been a commitment by development officers to view annual gifts of equal importance as one-time major gifts, says Truby. "Annual gifts help develop a habit of giving that sometimes one large donation can't do."

Sources: Jeanne L. Engle, Director of Development; Martha Truby, Associate Director of Annual Giving, Wisconsin Historical Foundation, Madison, WI. Phone (608) 264-6580 (Engle) Phone (608) 261-9363 (Truby) E-mail: jeanne.engle@wisconsinhistory.org E-mail: martha.truby@wisconsinhistory.org

Content not available in this edition

Content not available in this edition

Promotional Materials Encourage New $1,000 Donors

Materials promoting the $1,000 giving level, The Heritage Circle, of the Wisconsin Historical Foundation (Madison, WI) include brochures listing member benefits, right, and a letter of invitation.

Create Programs Aimed at Building Relationships

Use Special Events to Broaden Your Donor Pool

Too often, persons involved with managing major gift responsibilities dismiss planning and hosting special events, arguing, "They're too labor-intensive for the return we'll get."

On the contrary, the right special events — organized by the right group of volunteers — can reach out to persons of wealth and introduce them to your charity. These events can be the single best way to grab the attention of prospective donors.

In planning your special event, follow these wealth-targeted principles:

1. **Involve the same types of people in planning and organizing your event that you hope to attract — those with wealth or ties to it.** Beyond the steering committee, identify additional opportunities involving such persons.

2. **Make it clear to committee members who your target audience will be.** Give them some direction in identifying events that will appeal to those with disposable income — wine-tasting, black-tie galas, tours of expensive homes, etc.

3. **Whatever event you choose, incorporate elements of uniqueness and drawing-card appeal.** Convince persons with celebrity status to be present. Don't underestimate the ability of location to attract attendees. Add exciting twists to traditional event activities (e.g., silent/live auction items, raffles, entertainment, dining).

4. **Don't undercharge attendees.** Although the number of attendees will diminish as the price of admittance goes up, remember who it is that you want to attract.

5. **Plan for an event that will build year after year.** Although the first year of your event will set the stage for subsequent years, begin with a framework that can be embellished as each year goes by.

Award Dinner Raises Significant Funds, Celebrates Leaders

Major annual events can bring awareness and valuable publicity to your mission while connecting you to people capable of providing significant financial support.

The 47ᵗʰ Annual Leaders in Management Award Dinner hosted by Pace University (New York, NY) on April 29 at the New York City landmark, Cipriani Wall Street, raised $605,000. The money will support Pace's student scholarship program, president-selected projects and general purposes.

"The proceeds from the event will count toward Pace's seven-year, $100 million Centennial Campaign goal, which we realized two months ahead of schedule," says Christine Meola, Pace's vice president for philanthropy.

The event, an annual tradition since 1962, celebrates the personal and professional accomplishments of industry and community leaders as well as the university's continued advancement and promising future, Meola says. "It also reunites alums and showcases our talented musical theater students, who have performed for each of the past three years."

This year's dinner honored magazine publishing magnate and alumnus David J. Pecker, and online advertising innovator Gurbaksh Chahal.

Presenting Pecker's award was long-time friend and business associate Donald Trump. Presenting Chahal's award was Bruce Bachenheimer, clinical professor of management, director of entrepreneurship and Wilson Center for Social Entrepreneurship Faculty Fellow, who first met Chahal when he asked him to speak at a university event.

The celebration drew 325 attendees, including Eric Hillman, CEO of Europa Sports Products and an American Media advertiser, whose table included several noteworthy television celebrities. CNBC Anchor Maria Bartiromo served as mistress of ceremonies.

Tickets for the black-tie event ranged from $250 for young alumni level to $750 for contributor, $1,250 for supporter and $2,500 for sponsor. Sponsor table packages ranged from $10,000 to $50,000. Registration included the option of making a contribution if the person was unable to attend.

The event began with regular and VIP receptions at 6 p.m. Dinner was at 7 p.m. "Each presenter introduced a video of the honoree's career," says Meola. "For Gurbaksh Chahal, an excerpt from his interview with Oprah was shown (http://video.yahoo.com/watch/3791663/10391122) including the part where Oprah refers to him as 'one of the youngest and also the wealthiest entrepreneurs on the planet Earth.'"

To promote the dinner, Pace officials nationally distributed a press release by BusinessWire, says Samuella R. Becker, assistant director of public information. The event, Becker says, "was also featured on online event calendars such as New York Social Diary, Charity Benefits and BizBash Masterplanner, and gossiped about by Rush & Molloy of the NY Daily News. The San Francisco Chronicle also profiled Mr. Chahal in a story that appeared on the front page of one of its sections, entitled Internet Star Chahal Getting Honorary Doctorate. We are now receiving requests for after-the-event photos."

Sources: Samuella R. Becker, Assistant Director of Public Information; Christine M. Meola, Vice President for Philanthropy, Pace University, New York, NY. Phone (212) 346-1095 (Becker) or (212) 346-1637 (Meola). E-mail: Sbecker2@pace.edu or cmeola@pace.edu

Trade Large Events for Intimate Gatherings

The annual fundraiser luncheon was an important donor acquisition vehicle, but expensive, says Michele Berard, director of funds development at Butler Hospital (Providence, RI). The event collected over $130,000 but netted only around $10,000.

So when corporate sponsorship fell in 2008, staff decided to drop the luncheon in favor of smaller cultivation events. The shift in strategy was potentially risky but paid off handsomely, with $1.2 million raised the next year.

Several factors led to the breakthrough, says Berard. The more individualized format played a role, as did a shift from general operating expenses to an endowed research fund. But leveraging the connections of board members was the key development.

"We asked them to hold gatherings in their homes and invite people they knew could help the hospital with major donations," she explains. "Some were hesitant, but we told them that all they had to provide was their friends — the development office would do the rest."

Accordingly, staff assembled packets of prospective donor information, ensured that doctors and administrators attended meetings to answer questions and concerns, and even produced a 12-minute video featuring hospital research projects.

But perhaps most labor-intensive is the follow-up work staff does with contacts.

No direct solicitation is made at the events, says Berard. Instead, the video presentation ends with a general appeal, and not until later are contacts called to discuss specific commitments.

Seven cultivation events have been held since the summer of 2009, resulting in gifts ranging from $1,000 to $20,000, with one outstanding contribution of $100,000. And significantly, the $1 million-plus already raised has come from just 70 gifts.

Source: Michele Berard, Director of Funds Development, Butler Hospital, Providence, RI. Phone (401) 455-6581.
E-mail: mrberard@butler.org

Feed Your Board Members, Don't Eat Them

Board members are like chickens, says Michele Berard, director of funds development at Butler Hospital (Providence, RI). "You can eat your chickens to get the nourishment you need," Berard says, "but a much more sustainable approach is to give your chickens what they need to lay eggs for you."

The thrust of the analogy is clear: Board giving is important, but board getting is crucial. To move beyond a single-minded focus on board members' treasure, Berard suggests refining the definition of board fundraising duties.

"Opening your home to others, putting staff in touch with friends, inviting acquaintances to events — it all counts as getting" she says. "When people hear they don't have to actually ask for money, they breathe a big sigh of relief. And then they are much more willing to help."

Launch a Business-of-the-month Program

Looking for ways to make inroads with the business community? Launch a business-of-the-month awards program. Here's how:

1. **Assemble a committee.** Enlist a committee made up of business representatives who are already loyal supporters of your nonprofit. Charge them with overseeing the program and making nominations for the award.

2. **Identify qualifying businesses.** Give the committee a list of businesses in your area whose services or good works somehow compliment your organization's mission.

3. **Make monthly awards.** Based on the committee's nominations — and the criteria you provide — honor one business each month with a public presentation of the award that includes favorable publicity for the honored business.

4. **Host an annual event.** At the end of the year, invite all 12 award recipients and the public to an event that recognizes all chosen businesses and announce the business of the year selected from that group. Seek business support to sponsor the event cost.

This concept allows you to: 1) provide deserved recognition to businesses whose services or deeds support your mission, 2) build relationships with businesses that may become supportive of your work (e.g., donations, in-kind services, partnerships), and 3) gain visibility for your organization throughout the community and surrounding area.

Relationships Bloom With Executive Offerings

Consider creating a giving venue for a select group of your current or future supporters.

At Make-A-Wish Foundation of Illinois (Chicago, IL), Susan Schultze, manager of annual and leadership giving, and her colleagues were looking for a way to boost their individual giving when they developed their Executives for Make-A-Wish Network.

"Our individual giving was one of the areas we wanted to increase, and we were looking for a way to find people who have the heart for Make-A-Wish and the capacity to support our mission," Schultze explains.

So they decided to reach out to executives from companies that were already supporting the foundation, asking them each to make a $15,000 commitment over a three-year period to grant the wishes of three local children. Foundation representatives asked for the gifts to be personal gifts from the individual executives, hoping to use the network as a platform to transition members to longer-term individual giving.

"The idea to offer business forums and networking opportunities was taken straight from our local economic club," says Schultze. "They have these amazing business forums that are highly attended because of the speakers and the topics. We thought we could offer something similar, giving those who committed to the network access to other leaders in the community, along with high visibility for them as professionals supporting our organization."

Members of Make-A-Wish's executive network receive invitations to two gatherings per year that foster networking and give members access to other successful executives. They also receive invitations to the foundation's VIP and exclusive donor receptions, along with exposure for them as professionals in program booklets for the Wish Ball Gala, golf outing and donor luncheon events.

One third of the executives invited attended the network's initial meeting, with 11 committing to the network within the first year, raising $165,000 for the foundation, Schultze says. In addition, one of the executives generated another $50,000 in leads.

Funds raised made it possible for 33 children with life-threatening medical conditions to have their wishes granted through the foundation.

Source: Susan Schultze, Annual and Leadership Giving, Make-A-Wish Foundation of Illinois, Chicago, IL. Phone (312) 602-9427. E-mail: schultze@wishes.org

---

Ongoing Evaluation Important in Executive Network

While the initial offering of the Executives for Make-A-Wish Network was successful, Susan Schultze, manager of annual and leadership giving, Make-A-Wish Foundation of Illinois (Chicago, IL), says the program's ongoing success depends on continual evaluation of which executives are good prospects for individual versus corporate giving and whether the two types of giving can be separated.

Schultze and her colleagues have determined that many executives initially involved through the corporate program detailed above ultimately continue to support the organization and have a significant tie to the mission.

However, she says, the internal analysis also shows these executives tend to make their gifts through their company, allowing them to highlight their company involvement and supporting the organization at the same time. Plus, some executives had been making gifts at higher levels through their workplace giving programs prior to joining the network.

Schultze says this kind of evaluation ensures that the Make-A-Wish outreach and cultivation is accomplishing its goals. It also offers the opportunity to determine if there is a better way to engage those individuals.

"The Executives for Make-A-Wish Network did engage a few new people and offered existing supporters an additional way to engage," she notes. "Since the inception of the network, we have worked with these executives one-on-one to create partnerships that make sense on both sides of the table."

Courting the Wealthy, Second Edition.
Edited by Scott C. Stevenson.
© 2010 Stevenson, Inc. Published 2010 by Stevenson, Inc.

Cultivate & Engage Your Board

A financially-capable board should set the bar for gifts that follow. Board gifts can account for as much as 50 percent of a capital campaign goal, so it's critical that each board member be cultivated in highly personal ways. While some relationship-building moves may be the same as you would use with other would-be donors, some are more unique to this special group of individuals. Even engaging board members in helping you generate gifts from others serves as ways to cultivate them toward the realization of major gifts.

Teach Board Members to Nurture Relationships

Board members can play a powerful role in making introductions and cultivating relationships on your organization's behalf.

To make them more aware of their potential and assume a more proactive role in making introductions and cultivating major gift prospects, follow these steps:

1. Regularly share lists of nondonor prospects with board members. Ask them to select names of individuals, businesses and/or foundations they are willing to cultivate in various ways.

2. Share examples of board members or other volunteers who took the time to introduce your charity, particularly those introductions that eventually resulted in major gifts.

3. Make board members aware that you, or another staff person, are ready and willing to accompany board members on visits to would-be donors.

4. Encourage working in pairs if they find doing so more comfortable or productive.

5. Compliment board members who are performing and producing as expected. Do so in the presence of other board members.

Get One Board Member Who Will Champion Your Cause

If your nonprofit has little history of securing major gifts, one of the most important steps you can take is to enlist a financially capable board member who knows and is respected by others of means. If that person does nothing more than to help identify and attract other board members, he/she will have made a significant contribution to your cause.

Here's one approach for enlisting such an individual:

1. First, review your inner circle of most generous contributors. Who among them already has an affinity to the work of your charity? Your champion will hopefully reside within this group. If not, you may need to look for another who has a history of philanthropy to other causes within your community and begin to cultivate his/her interest. This latter option may have equal potential to the first but will require more time nurturing his/her interest and involvement.

2. Begin meeting individually with your top three or four choices. Explain that your goal is to bring someone of his/her stature on board with the sole intent of

identifying, cultivating and enlisting others of means to join your board or to eventually make a major gift.

3. As you meet with each potential champion, be up front and specific about your expectations: "I would like you to give at least one year of your time — meeting on a monthly basis — to identify and cultivate 10 individuals who have the capability of making $10,000-and-above gifts to our charity."

4. Once an individual has agreed to work with you, meet regularly to review names and discuss possible approaches for each prospect the two of you identify. Offer to accompany your champion on calls, but be clear that he/she will be key at making introductions and being involved in the friend-building process.

By following this procedure with one willing individual throughout the course of a year, you will be building a foundation that will eventually result in attracting capable individuals who will one day invest generously in your cause.

Nurture the Few Who Will Raise the Bar

Want to convince more board members to give at higher levels? Focus your cultivation efforts on those few board members who possess the capacity and proclivity to give more generously.

If you build a group of board members committed to major gifts, their example will motivate remaining board members to do more.

Whether your attention is geared to a particular board member or a few, here's how to get them to step up to the plate:

1. Get that board member to establish a sizeable challenge

gift to match new and increased gifts from other board members.

2. After he/she makes a large gift, convince that board member to be your spokesperson who encourages fellow board members to give at higher levels or get off the board.

3. Engage board members in identifying a funding project that the full board can buy into and realize through their collective gifts.

Ask Every Board Member to Give You Exposure

To make new contacts with persons of wealth, be proactive in asking board members to include you in get-togethers with their friends and associates. Your simple presence could open doors leading to further meetings.

Extend an invitation for board members to think how they might include you as a friend in group get-togethers. Share some examples of how that might occur:

- Joining them as a guest at some other nonprofit's fundraiser.

- Accompanying them to a chamber of commerce event.

- Inviting you to join a foursome in a round of golf.

- Inclusion on their guest list for private dinner parties and receptions.

- Accompanying them to civic club meetings.

- Introductions to their company's top decision makers.

In addition, encourage board members to ask their spouses to include you in group gatherings if and when appropriate.

Instruct Board Members to Introduce You and Your Cause

Do you have a method to encourage board members to introduce you and your organization to individuals, businesses and foundations?

If your board is made up of movers and shakers, they should be in positions to help introduce your organization and assist in the cultivation of prospects. And for those board members who shudder at the thought of asking people for money, you can assure them that their primary role is simply to help make introductions and cultivate friendships. If necessary, you or another advancement official can be prepared to make any asks.

Formalize your procedure for involving board members in this friend-making process by developing a form similar to the example shown to the right. At a regularly scheduled board meeting, ask board members to complete it and return it to you within a specified number of days. Then be prepared to begin following up with each board member immediately. (It's important to act while the assignment is still fresh in his/her mind.)

When you distribute the form, be sure to include your last honor roll of contributors so board members will be sure not to include names of those who are presently contributing to your organization. Better yet, also include a list of nondonors who would be likely prospect candidates.

FRIEND-MAKING OBJECTIVES FOR BOARD MEMBERS
Confidential

The purpose of this project is to involve all board members in making introductions and cultivating relationships with nondonors capable of making gifts of $10,000 or more. Your ability to help establish a positive relationship with friends and associates will help broaden our base of future major gift support as we plan for the future.

Our goal is to make individual introductory visits with each person you have identified within the next three months. Subsequent visits and objectives will be determined once initial calls have been completed.

Please identify three or more prospects (individuals, businesses or foundations) — who are presently not donors — capable of contributing $10,000 or more to our organization. We ask that you complete this form within the next week and return it to [Name].

Once your form is received, the appropriate development officer will contact you to begin coordinating available dates and times to set appointments with the persons you have identified.

Your Name _____ Date_____

1. Prospect _____

Your Relationship to the Prospect: _____
Helpful Background Information (e.g., occupation, title, source of wealth): _____

2. Prospect _____

Your Relationship to the Prospect: _____
Helpful Background Information:_____
_____

3. Prospect _____
Your Relationship to the Prospect: _____
Helpful Background Information:_____
_____

Create a Traveling Ambassador Corps to Assist in Cultivation

Do you have a board member making a business trip to the East or West Coast?

What about that retired board member who vacations in Florida each winter? Turn these and other close friends of your organization into traveling ambassadors by involving them in cultivating major gift prospects who live at or near their travel destinations.

These traveling ambassadors can help do their part to enhance the image and work of your organization throughout the nation.

Use an anticipated trips form such as the one at right to pinpoint opportunities to involve persons in identifying, cultivating, researching and even soliciting gifts on your behalf.

In their travels, these persons could assist you by:

- Hosting a reception.
- Conducting prospect research on individuals, businesses or foundations in that region.
- Making introductory calls.
- Delivering a message of thanks for past support.
- Hand-delivering a proposal.
- Seeking donated items for events.

Rather than sending or e-mailing forms, distribute them at board meetings to explain how helpful members' involvement can be with these out-of-town prospects. Share the forms selectively on a one-to-one basis with others who travel in affluent circles.

When you receive a completed form, identify appropriate fund development activities and discuss them with the person submitting the form before departure.

Sharing this form will have multiple benefits:

- Completed forms help keep your office posted on the schedules of board members and others.
- By involving these persons in the fund development process, you are also engaging them — helping them more fully own the role of major gifts at your institution.
- Their involvement will help realize cultivation, research and solicitation that otherwise might not have been accomplished.

RANDOM UNIVERSITY
Anticipated Trips Form

This form is for board members and other Random University insiders who wish to serve as ambassadors during their business and leisure travels.

When a trip is planned, simply complete this form and turn it in to the Institutional Advancement Office. A development officer will contact you to go over possible ways in which you could assist in making contacts with individuals. Thank you!

Name _____

Trip Destination _____
❑ Business   ❑ Pleasure

Trip Arrival Date _____ Departure Date _____

Where You Can Be Reached During Trip:
Address _____ E-mail _____
Phone (_____) _____ Fax _____

Examples of Ambassador activities with which you might assist:

❑ Introductory visits:
    ❑ With individuals
    ❑ With business representatives
    ❑ With foundations

❑ Friendship-building activities
❑ Distributing literature about Random University
❑ Hosting a reception
❑ Identifying potential contributors
❑ Telephoning friends/donors of the university
❑ Soliciting a gift
❑ Delivering a proposal
❑ Securing donated items for our annual gala
❑ Other (Please describe) _____
_____
_____

Board Cultivation Idea

At least once a year, provide each board member with an individual tour of your facilities, allowing him/her to observe your nonprofit in action. Occasionally stop and visit with an employee and pose a question about the employee's work.

This process allows board members to see your organization in action and witness its important work while helping to uncover individual funding interests of these key players.

Leverage the Powerful Reputations of Your Board Members

Board members articulate strategic direction, provide organizational continuity and often supply their share of elbow grease to a nonprofit's mission. But beyond the services they provide, their reputation in the local, regional or national community can be of great benefit as well.

Larry Stybel understands how boards operate inside and out. He is cofounder and vice president of Board Options, Inc. (Boston, MA) — a nationally recognized company specializing in helping boards be effective problem-solving units through the application of practical behavioral science — and executive in residence at the Sawyer School of Business at Suffolk University (Boston, MA).

Here, Stybel shares his expertise in the art of leveraging the reputation of prestigious board members:

What is the central rationale behind showcasing well-known board members?

"Donors, when they were children, were told by their mothers that they would be known by the company they keep. This is what board members do for nonprofits. If you are an up-and-coming nonprofit that does not have top-flight status, one way to create reputation and cache is through your board members. In branded institutions like MIT or Princeton, the institution gives luster to the board member. But in smaller organizations, the opposite is true: board members lend their credibility to the nonprofit."

So in attracting donors and other prospective board members...

"Prestigious board members function like the anchor store of a shopping center, the place that all the other shops cluster around. If a brand-name person is on your board, other people will want to be associated with that individual, and, by extension, your organization and its mission."

Are there any challenges to having well-known board members?

"If you are not a prestigious institution, there is a limit to how many brand-name people you can afford to have on your board. Two is great; six might not be so great. One of the disadvantages of bright star board members is that they often have only limited time to put into your organization. They will not typically be the shirtsleeves board members who dig in and really get things done. Bright stars are important, but they are prone to fighting with each other, and too many can be counterproductive."

What should organizations know about using the name of a bright star board member?

"That it should always be done with the knowledge and agreement of the board member. That individual is lending his or her name and stature to your organization, and you don't want to abuse that privilege. A bright star should never find out you used his name after the fact. And also be aware that if he is a CEO or president, his business will often want to clear the use of the name beforehand as well."

Is there anything a shirtsleeves-heavy board should do or not do in looking for bright star members?

"One tip is to make board participation a finite commitment. Prestigious individuals don't want to be trapped on the board of a smaller nonprofit forever, even if they believe in its mission. Setting a term limit of two or three years spares them the awkwardness of resigning and makes them more likely to agree to the initial commitment."

Source: Larry Stybel, Co-Founder and Vice President, Board Options, Inc., Boston, MA. Phone (617) 594-7627. E-mail: Lstybel@boardoptions.com

Host a Reception for All Past Board Members

Many nonprofits give former board members emeritus status as a way to keep them involved after their terms end. Unfortunately, far more nonprofits do little or nothing to maintain that relationship with former board members.

If your nonprofit has let relationships with former board members slide, why not coordinate an event geared just for them? Here's how you might do that:

1. Pull together a committee made up of current and former board members, and charge them with coordinating a board appreciation event.
2. Suggest that the committee schedule an event with some drawing card appeal — perhaps at a to-die-for home that visitors would love to visit.
3. In addition to plenty of social time, incorporate a brief program that brings past board members up to speed on your nonprofit's current happenings. In fact, you might want to ask these former board members if they would like the group to continue on a more formal basis, perhaps meeting twice a year or quarterly.

If the group of former board members agrees to form a more official capacity, you may want to involve them in any number of fund development activities.

Stay Connected With Former Board Members

Developing strong relationships with current board members is key to staying connected with them — and keeping them engaged with and supporting your organization — after they retire.

"There is a greater chance of keeping former board members engaged if they were developed and cultivated during their tenure on the board," says Diane Dean, principal, The Dean Consulting Group (Rutherford, NJ). "There is a unique advantage to having informed insight regarding board members' interests, talents, skills and reasons for committing to the organization on a volunteer leadership level."

Tools to develop and sustain relationships include personal questionnaires, self-assessments and committee evaluations, plus activities at orientations and board retreats.

Forming a board development committee to recruit, engage and develop board members is another useful strategy.

"The best board strategies, the ones that get results that can be tracked to prove success, are those that are incorporated as programs with written procedures and a clear goal of what success looks like," says Paul Nazareth, manager of planned and personal giving, Catholic Archdiocese of Toronto (Toronto, Ontario, Canada).

A well-crafted communications plan should include a formal recognition process for people coming on and off the board.

"One innovative idea I've seen is an organization that will add a recommendation to a board member's LinkedIn profile if he or she fulfills the top five criteria of an excellent board member (make a commitment to the board, volunteer in programs, advocate in the community, network for the organization, make a leadership or planned gift)," Nazareth says.

One way to engage retiring board members that is often overlooked is to simply ask them what level of involvement they would like and whether that involvement would occur immediately after the end of their board service or in a few years.

Sources: Diane D. Dean, Principal, The Dean Consulting Group, Rutherford, NJ. Phone (800) 686-1975.
E-mail: ddean@thedeanconsultinggroup.com.
Website: www.thedeanconsultinggroup.com
Paul Nazareth, Manager, Planned and Personal Giving at Catholic Archdiocese of Toronto, Toronto, Ontario, Canada.
Phone (416) 934-3411. E-mail: pnazareth@archtoronto.org.
Website: www.archtoronto.org

Involvement Opportunities That Lead to Investment

Cultivation is all about the five I's — identification, information, interest, involvement and finally, investment. Following are several examples of ways in which you can involve and engage would-be donors in the life of your organization.

Advisory Boards Welcome Involvement, Lead to Major Gifts

Identify and mine specific ways to connect individuals, businesses and industries to your organization to engage them in your cause.

Purdue University (West Lafayette, IN) hosts 34 industrial advisory boards that share research with corporate partners and build relationships that lead to funding.

Each advisory board is tied to a different field of research, such as food sciences, computer science, engineering education, and computer information and technology, says Betsy Liley, assistant vice president for corporate and foundation relations.

Liley says many of the boards are structured around membership levels, which range from $2,500 to $80,000 per year. Average group size is 15 to 20. These annual gifts help pay for the costs of running each board, including a salary for a paid staff member.

In addition to the annual membership gift, many companies sponsor research projects and fund scholarships for students in fields of interest to their advisory board, Liley says. While individual board structures vary, generally, each board sponsors research as a group, attends two meetings a year and may participate in annual job recruitment fairs.

"If the company's interest is in students and recruiting, they will be interested in supporting scholarships that will get them in front of students," she says. "If their interest is in research, they will want to sponsor research projects that expose them to our experts and allow them direct access to our research."

Advisory board members are at the corporate management level. Specific departments or colleges — many of which already have relationships with those departments or colleges through previous research funding — identify prospective corporate partners or attendance at job recruitment fairs on campus.

"Corporate involvement helps shape our curriculum, keeps us up to date on the skills our students need to have to compete in the job market, and guides our research," says Liley. "Our corporate partners have access to our research and our top students, and get to interact with their peers and partner with them on projects."

Source: Betsy Liley, Assistant Vice President for Corporate & Foundation Relations, Purdue University, West Lafayette, IN. Phone (765) 494-0635. E-mail: bliley@purdue.edu

Content not available in this edition

Involvement Opportunities That Lead to Investment

Recruit, Manage a Major Gifts Advisory Committee

Just because your development office is small doesn't mean you can't raise big gifts.

Follow these steps to create a volunteer-driven major gifts advisory committee that will expand your efforts in identifying, researching, cultivating and soliciting significant gifts:

1. Begin by developing a written job description for your group and presenting it to your board for approval. It's important to get board buy-in for your major gifts program. In fact, include board representation on your committee.

2. Recruit a small group — say five to eight individuals who have either made a significant gift to your charity or have the ability to make a major gift — to serve a one-

or two-year term on the committee. Look for those with connections to wealth.

3. Meet for up to two hours a month to begin a system of: 1) building a manageable list of major gift prospects, 2) prioritizing prospects based on financial capability and proclivity to give, 3) developing individual cultivation plans for each, 4) determining who should meet with whom and 5) knowing assignments for the month ahead.

4. Develop a printed description of five or six gift opportunities for you and the advisory committee to share with prospects as cultivation becomes more intense and focused.

5. Use subsequent meetings to report progress and decide on next steps.

Involve, Engage Major Donors

Staff with the California Institute of Technology (Pasadena, CA) ask alumni, philanthropists and people interested in various areas of science to serve on committees that advise six academic divisions in the hope they will give and help get money.

The academic divisions are physics, math and astronomy; chemistry and chemical engineering; biology; engineering; information science technology; and geology and planetary science. Plans are to add divisions that represent cross-disciplinary initiatives, says Peter Hero, vice president of development and institute relations.

The committee-driven idea came from board members who understand fundraising is about engaging donors, Hero says, noting that the first committee, developed two years ago, has already contributed $1.5 million.

Each committee includes a board trustee, academic department chair, senior development officer, donors and prospective donors. Committees meet twice a year for dinner and a day of discussions about the academic division's priorities.

"New committee members are given job descriptions and a clear understanding of the structure of the meetings," says Hero. "We want them to interact with each other and to

meet students." The development chair leaves the meeting with a to-do list, including names of prospective members to contact. Committee members spend four to six hours over the next six months making phone calls and communicating by e-mail with staff.

Only one of the committees asks members to give an annual gift, he says. The others focus on the priorities of the academic division and finding potential funders. "We want them to open their Rolodex and reach out to their network for support," he says.

While senior development officers have been able to manage the committees so far, Hero says that as support and visibility for projects grow, and the need for special analysis and fundraising strategies emerges, staff support may also grow.

The committees have been an effective way to build donor support and also connect donors with each other, says Hero, "In this way, giving becomes less of a singular act and more of a joint effort."

Source: Peter Hero, Vice President of Development & Institute Relations, California Institute of Technology, Pasadena, CA. Phone (626) 395-6307. E-mail: phero@caltech.edu

Strategic Planning Procedures

■ Since not everyone can be invited to a strategic planning process, share a confidential summary of your meeting — stamped "Draft" — with select prospects who were not in attendance and get their reactions to it before preparing the final document.

Seek Key Donors' Input

If you're in the process of gearing up for a capital campaign, revamping your website or testing new collaterals, be sure to get your key donors involved in the process.

Asking donors for their opinion takes very little time and can garner useful feedback for you. It also makes donors feel as if they are making a positive contribution to the organization — one that's not monetary — and fosters good will.

Involve Key Players With Outreach Efforts

It's not uncommon for development professionals to hit the road prior to and during a capital campaign. Sometimes referred to as the chicken dinner circuit, a charity may host a number of events in key areas throughout regions or cities in which constituent populations are concentrated.

These outreach cultivation efforts are the perfect time to engage key donors and prospects. Helping them gain ownership of your fundraising efforts will help to maximize their eventual financial investment. And persons of means and reputation involved in a volunteer capacity will help your organization attract others also capable of making generous gifts.

Here are but a few ways to involve donor hopefuls who reside in the communities in which you're planning group cultivation efforts:

1. Ask them to host a reception in their homes, places of business or exclusive club, particularly if the location has drawing-card appeal for invitees.

2. Involve them in developing the guest list, providing them with a printout of existing names, addresses, phone numbers and links to your organization. Encourage them to add their own contacts to the list.

3. Invite them to accompany development officers on a few follow-up calls to key prospects — individuals, businesses or foundations — during the days after your group event.

4. Ask them to serve on a planning committee, enlist committee members or sign their names on the letter of invitation.

5. Invite them to provide testimonials at some point during your group event.

6. Elevate their involvement to a level that requires them to travel to your facilities at least once a year, engaging them even more in their ownership of your organization and its work.

Involve Donors in Methods to Advance Donor Relations

Here's a way to learn improved ways of dealing with donors:

Invite some existing donors to meet with your development staff. Use the time to discuss ways of improving donor relations — acknowledgment letters, e-mail communications, preferred or new ways for setting and confirming appointments and more.

Here are examples of questions you may wish to pose:

- How do you feel about the timeliness of gift acknowledgments?
- How do you react to their contents?

- What have other charities done for you (as a donor) that impressed you?
- What have other charities done that you found offensive?
- How could we improve our way of approaching you for support?

Not only will answers to these and other questions provide valuable insight into improving donor relations, you will also be utilizing a new and valuable cultivation strategy with those interviewed.

Set Brainstorming Sessions With Donors, Would-be Donors

Looking for ways to involve high-end donors and probable donors? Seek their input on major gift issues.

Schedule a series of small-group brainstorming sessions that include both donors and would-be donors. Do it over breakfast or lunch or dinner to attract their participation, and have the invitation come from your CEO. You may even choose to ask board members or prominent donors to host sessions at their homes or offices.

After a brief introduction to explain the meeting's purpose and why the guests were invited, pose one or two key questions to the group and ask them to share their ideas. Have a staff person take notes to show you take their responses seriously.

Examples of questions may include:

✓ What steps can we take to forge relationships with people and businesses who have the ability to invest significantly in our organization and those we serve?

✓ How can we do a better job of reaching out to community leaders?

✓ How can we make community leaders more aware of and excited about the funding project I just described?

You may be pleasantly surprised by the responses you receive and the direction these sessions take. Engaging both donors and would-be donors will encourage greater ownership of fundraising efforts.

Points to Consider in Forming An Endowment Committee

To generate more endowment gifts, consider the merits of forming an endowment committee that includes representation from your board of trustees and non-board members who are affluent or have connections to persons of affluence.

Once your endowment committee is assembled, charge its members with meeting monthly or quarterly to:

- Identify endowment prospects and develop cultivation strategies for each.

- With staff input, develop a wish list of naming endowment opportunities.

- Explore targeted ways of marketing endowment opportunities.

- Make select cultivation and/or solicitation calls on prospects.

- Shape strategies to urge those with existing endowments to add to them.

- Develop a stewardship plan that keeps existing donors updated and informed about the impact of their gifts.

Invite Potential Donors to Identify Future Achievements

Do you have an up-to-date strategic plan? Did the planning process include involving those whom you're counting on for major gifts?

A part of prospects' involvement time should be devoted to identifying future accomplishments based on your mission and services. Asking participants to identify what they perceive as future accomplishments helps to do so while also providing insight into their funding interests. Use these questions to help flush out participants' loftiest future achievements for your organization:

- Five years from now, our city's newspaper has a front-

page story about a major accomplishment of our agency. What's the headline? How does it read?

- Our organization has just received a million-dollar gift. How will that million dollars have been used and what will it be accomplishing five years from now?

- Identify what you perceive to be the single biggest challenge facing our community — within the scope of our agency's mission and programs — and then describe what our agency accomplished, over a five-year period, to address that challenge.

Form Ambassador Clusters In Neighboring Communities

If your nonprofit serves communities outside of your city, form ambassador groups in those areas to assist with fund development. To get such groups up and running:

1. Ask persons in surrounding communities who already support your cause to join that community's ambassador advisory group. To encourage their involvement, explain that the group's purpose goes far beyond fund development. In addition to assisting with prospect identification, cultivation, solicitation and stewardship of current donors, they will be expected to make the public more aware of the positive ways in which your organization

serves the community.

2. Have each community's group meet quarterly to learn more about your organization and to plan and support activities for that community: host an educational program, plan a special event or after-hours reception, identify and review names of prospective donors, plan stewardship calls to thank other current donors and more.

Over time, the attention you give to forming and supporting the efforts of ambassador groups in those communities you serve will result in broadening the level of support for your organization.

Involvement Opportunities That Lead to Investment

Link Traveling Ambassadors with Faraway Prospects

Take a look at your donor list. Which persons on the list travel for business or personal pleasure on a regular basis?

Why not develop a plan to involve these traveling friends as ambassadors for your organization? Invite them to link up with both prospects and donors who live far from your institution. Properly trained, these traveling ambassadors can assist with identifying, researching, cultivating, soliciting and stewarding faraway constituents.

Follow this step-by-step process to secure and train traveling ambassadors:

1. Enlist two or three existing donors who travel regularly and would be willing to serve as ambassadors on behalf of your organization.

2. With this core committee, review a list of other donors who travel and devise a plan to approach them to determine if any would be willing to join your committee of traveling ambassadors.

3. As your committee grows, meet monthly or quarterly to review names of faraway prospects and donors based on geographic regions. As individual committee members indicate their intent to visit particular cities or regions, invite them to phone or visit face-to-face with persons from those areas. As committee members agree to make calls, outline specific objectives for each person with whom they plan to meet (e.g. thank for a previous gift, update on happenings at your charity, etc.).

4. Following each meeting, send individual memos to each committee member who reconfirms who he/she is to call on, when, and the objective of the call. You can provide additional background information on those to be seen with this memo. Also include trip report forms (and any additional materials for the ambassador to distribute to prospects/donors).

5. Instruct ambassadors that their completed trip reports include any follow up to be conducted by your office. You may discover as a result of the visit, for instance, that the timing would be appropriate for solicitation, or a family member's death requires a gesture of sympathy from your nonprofit. The completed trip report will point out what needs to happen next.

6. Finally, as your committee continues to meet, keep members informed on the status of those with whom each has visited. Doing so will help to keep them motivated as owners of the solicitation process.

Develop a form such as this to review names of prospects/ donors and determine who will call on whom during the next three-month period.

COMMITTEE OF TRAVELING AMBASSADORS

Long-distance Donors/Prospects to Be Seen

Name	City/State	Relationship	Proposed Objective	Caller	Target Date
M/M Mark Andrews	Cleveland/OH	Prospect/'55 Alum	Rate/screen for major gift	Wilson	02/11
Sarah Gailey	Cleveland/OH	Son attended Postum/Donor	Thank for past support	Wilson	02/11
GoMark Inc./Sands	San Diego/CA	'62 Alum/Donor	Update on scholarship	Hadley	03/11
Bremer Foundation	San Diego/CA	Prospect	Intro/secure guidelines	——	
Allison/Mike Gentry	San Diego/CA	'71/'71 Alums/Donors	Thanks for recent gift	Hadley	03/11
Dr. Claude Everist	San Diego/CA	Emeritus Board Member	Update on strategic plan	Hadley	03/11
Ian Smith	Los Angeles/CA	Former Student/Prospect	Research	——	
Mattie Christensen	Riverside/CA	'43 Alum/Planned Gift	Thank and update	Nelson	02/11
Tom Eisenburg	Los Angeles/CA	'49 Alum/Donor	Solicit for Annual Fund	Nelson	02/11
Melony/Tim Winchell	Kansas City/MO	'72/'74 Alums/Prospects	Share wish list	Hinton	01/11
Hallmark Foundation	Kansas City/MO	Prospect	Intro/secure guidelines	Hinton	01/11
Tina Marie Noonan	Liberty/MO	Former Student/Prospect	Intro/research	Hinton	01/11

Cultivating Planned Gifts

Because planned gifts are generally realized after the donor's lifetime, the approaches used to build relationships with planned gift donors may vary in some ways from those used to secure outright gifts. In addition to cultivating donors, it's also important to cultivate relationships with agents of wealth: attorneys, trust officers, CPAs, financial planners and others.

Look for Clues and Signals From Donors

Be on the lookout for clues and signals from annual gift donors who may want to do more and include your organization in their estate plans. Look for these three signals:

1. **Those who are always there.** Look for those people who always show up at events — those friends and supporters who keep coming to every event you host. Those are people in which you need to pay attention.

2. **Those who pay you a visit.** The people who come into your facility or office when they don't have to may be trying to tell you something. They may be seeking your attention for any number of reasons.

3. **Donors who include personal notes with gifts.** Notes that are included with their annual gift could be a clue that these donors want to do more. They're giving you signals that they're interested in your organization and may want to explore additional ways of investing in your cause.

Work to Identify and Cultivate Children of Wealth

It's common for most nonprofits to focus on those with existing wealth. To lay the groundwork for major gifts that may not materialize for 10 or 20 years, develop a plan aimed at cultivating children of wealth.

Your community is full of individuals in their 30s, 40s and even 50s who are not yet in positions that enable them to make five- or six-figure gifts but will be in 10 or 20 years by virtue of their positions or inherited wealth.

Begin to cultivate those up-and-comers now with a plan that's unique to your organization. Here's one generic scenario that helps illustrate how to do it:

1. Launch some sort of young leaders society that is exclusive to 30- to 50-year-olds who contribute $1,000 or more annually to your organization.

2. Create a steering committee made of those donors who can take ownership in the effort and design a plan that caters to the interests of this age group. The steering committee can come up with social activities, member perks, donor recognition ideas, etc.

3. Encourage the committee to establish an annual awards program that recognizes its members in various categories (e.g., professional achievement, philanthropic efforts, volunteer contributions, etc.).

When members turn 51, induct them into a more traditional, inclusive $1,000-and-above gift club. Hold an annual graduation ceremony that welcomes them into the older crowd.

Planned Gift Triggers

■ Key life events can cause donors to think about planned giving. Events that can trigger the desire for estate planning include the birth of a child or grandchild, the death of a friend or relative or the retirement of the donor.

Be Prompt and Thorough

When a donor or would-be donor contacts you to get an answer to a question, make it standard practice to get a complete response back to him/her within 24 hours. This will elevate your professional credibility.

Conduct a Winning Interview With a Planned Gift Prospect

Conversations with planned gift prospects should be donor-centered and stress donor benefits using assets that will be a problem to dispose of or distribute now or in the future, says Pamela Jones Davidson, president, Davidson Gift Design (Bloomington, IN).

"The gift is not the most important goal during a meeting with a planned gift prospect," she says. "The most important goal is to empower the prospect to see the opportunity for a gift that they can understand and even make. Harvey DeVries (a pioneer in planned giving, and the first person to write a charitable remainder trust) said the role of the gift planner is to help donors figure out how to make a gift.

"When I meet with planned gift prospects, I ask them, 'Would you (prospect name) consider making a gift if we could show you how?'"

You can't raise planned gifts without personal discussions with people about planned gift options, says Davidson. "Listen for the 'I'd like to give, but...' statement and use that information to help donors find a way to fulfill their goals.

"For everything someone lists as an impediment to making a gift, there is a planned gift or charitable plan that will meet or exceed his or her goal," the planned gift expert says. "For example, if a prospect says, 'I'd like to give, but my No. 1 goal is to provide for my surviving spouse,'

your reply could be, 'There are many ways to do that, such as charitable plans that pay income, like gift annuities or charitable remainder trusts.'

"At the end of a meeting with a planned gift prospect, I say, 'We talked about a lot of different options today. Let me send you a recap of those options in writing that you can share with your financial advisor,'" says Davidson. "Go home and recap everything in a letter, including what that donor has told you about their planning goals, and send it to the prospect. Put a copy of the letter in the prospect's folder. This creates a historical record of your relationship with that donor that can be used by you, other development staff at your organization, and by your successor in future conversations with the prospect about that and other gifts."

Your goal should always be the best possible gift for the donor, not the best possible gift for your organization, she says.

"We tend to think we own prospects. How many of us give to only one charity? But when your message is that planned gifts will work for your charity and every other organization the prospect cares about, they're going to listen a lot more intently, and ethics are well-served."

Source: Pamela Jones Davidson, JD, President, Davidson Gift Design, Bloomington, IN. Phone (812) 876-8646. E-mail: pjdavidson@giftplanners.com

Build an Active, Accomplished Planned Gifts Committee

Many nonprofits take the time to form a planned gifts committee that meets occasionally but accomplishes little. That's a waste of everyone's time.

To build an active planned gifts committee, one whose members are really working to help promote and assist with planned gifts activities:

Make expectations clear. Develop a roles and responsibilities statement that sets forth both group and individual expectations for the members of your committee. Review those responsibilities with committee candidates prior to their appointments.

Assist your committee in setting yearly goals that include quantifiable objectives (e.g., to individually identify

and meet with no fewer than 10 planned gift prospects throughout the year).

Schedule regular meetings that include individual assignments. In addition to reviewing and approving planned gift policies, ask your chair to assign specific tasks to members (e.g., contacting prospects, calling on attorneys, participating in a planned gift seminar).

Give them the recognition they deserve. Devote a page to this group on your website, including photos and brief biographies. List their names on planned gift letterhead and in your planned gifts newsletter. Publicly introduce them at estate planning seminars and other related events.

Five Reasons for Distributing a Planned Gifts Newsletter

Ever wonder if the cost of a planned gifts newsletter is worth it? Here are five reasons why it pays to distribute a planned gifts newsletter to select prospects:

1. Those on your mailing list become increasingly knowledgeable of how types of charitable gifts work and the benefits of each.

2. Regular communication helps to position your charity in the minds of those who receive it.

3. Real-life examples and illustrations help readers more fully understand the impact of what their own planned gifts might accomplish.

4. The newsletters offer an additional avenue for recognizing those who have made planned gift commitments.

5. By including a return bounce back in every issue of your planned gifts newsletter, you can get answers to important questions such as: Have you included XYZ Charity in your estate plans? Would you like more information about planned gifts to XYZ Charity?

Planning Guidebooks Add Value to Donor Magazine

One proven way to engage major donors is to provide them with tools to achieve other desired goals while also supporting a worthy cause.

At Northwestern University Feinberg School of Medicine (Chicago, IL), development staff have produced a family-focused estate planning guidebook exploring ethical wills and methods for equitably distributing estate among children.

"Declining economic conditions shifted a lot of people's priorities away from charity and towards taking care of family first," says Joanna Riester, associate director of donor relations. "This booklet was chosen to show how people can take care of their loved ones and still further their ideals through charitable giving."

The guidebook is part of an ongoing series designed to augment the office's biannual donor magazine. Developed in collaboration with a third-party vendor, each booklet/magazine pairing shares a common theme and highlights a central topic such as a featured giving vehicle or timely piece of news.

While the booklets are distributed primarily to subscribers requesting further information, development staff use the booklets as well, Riester says, noting that the range of topics covered makes them a useful grab-and-go resource for development officers.

Much of the copy featured in guidebooks is provided by the vendor but can be tailored to specific donor stories or university events, says Riester. And while the materials cost $5,000 to $10,000 per issue (both guidebooks and magazine), Riester says she believes this is money well spent.

"Our donors are extremely generous, and we owe it to them to provide quality advice and planning options," she says. "These materials provide enough interest and substance to keep them turning the page and taking our next call."

Source: Joanna Riester, Associate Director of Donor Relations, Northwestern University, Feinberg School of Medicine Office of Development, Chicago, IL. Phone (312) 503-8933. E-mail: J-riester@northwestern.edu

Content not available in this edition

Nurture a League of Planned Gift Ambassadors

Although it requires a significant investment of time, building a volunteer group of planned gift ambassadors can significantly increase your ability to identify, cultivate and secure additional planned gifts for your organization.

Here's a framework for building a corps of planned gift ambassadors:

1. **Develop a three-year plan that outlines goals for your ambassador program.** How many volunteers would you like in place at the end of your first year? What communities or geographic locations would be ideal for the presence of these ambassadors?

2. **Methodically begin to recruit, train and support your ambassadors.** Invite those who have already chosen to make a planned gift to serve as ambassadors. Turn to professionals (attorneys, trust officers, insurance agents) in particular communities who have an existing connection to your cause.

3. **Provide your new recruits with a position description that shows what is expected of them** — to regularly identify, research, cultivate and assist in the solicitation of planned gift prospects.

4. **Work with and support each ambassador and ambassador group as circumstances dictate.** Take an ambassador on a call. Accompany an ambassador who is willing to introduce you to a new planned gift prospect. Meet with a community's ambassador group (which may amount to two or three individuals) to review activities and plan strategies.

Even if you only have three ambassador groups with three or four members in each group by the end of year one, you will have launched a volunteer effort that will expand and enhance your efforts to market planned gifts.

Nurture Attorney Ambassadors

Anyone with planned giving experience will tell you that having attorneys going to bat on behalf of your organization is helpful.

But how do you get attorneys on board? After all, attorneys will generally say that ethics prevent them from encouraging clients to make estate plans for a specific nonprofit. And that's true. However, when clients are the ones bringing up the topic of charitable gifts — seeking their attorney's advice — it's in your nonprofit's interest to have attorneys familiar with your cause and the many ways that you accept gifts.

Building a corps of attorney ambassadors is a long-term investment that requires building respect for both you and the institution you represent. With a system in place, you can set annual objectives that include adding and cultivating a minimum number of these professionals to your centers of influence list.

To build an attorney ambassador corps:

- Meet one-on-one with attorneys in your area to summarize your planned gift program and leave your business card. Stop by at least once a year to update them on your organization and examples of planned gifts you've received.

- Put those attorneys on your mailing list to receive your newsletter, magazine and planned gifts newsletter.

- Be sure your planned gifts advisory committee — and, if possible, board of trustees — include attorneys.

- Cultivate attorney relationships by including them in estate planning workshops for your constituency. If you coordinate workshops in other communities, recruit attorneys from those locations to assist with your effort.

- When you come across a charitable gift article that would interest your attorney ambassadors, send them a copy of it along with a personal note.

- Host a reception or luncheon for your agents of wealth. Have your CEO and other board members on hand to thank them for their interest in your cause. Cite examples of how planned gifts benefit those you serve.

- When your agency realizes planned gifts, don't overlook the attorneys involved in the distribution of assets. They will be much more amiable when future opportunities present themselves if they have had a previously pleasant relationship.

Invite Planned Gift Donors to Make Board Testimonials

You'd think that asking members of nonprofit boards to make planned gifts would be like preaching to the choir. But in reality, many nonprofit boards don't set the example they should be expected to when it comes to making planned gifts. If this is the case in your nonprofit, you may want to invite a willing planned gift donor to attend a regular board meeting to explain what motivated him/her to make a planned gift.

In addition to motivating board members to make planned gifts, the presentation of a planned gift donor before your board is a wonderful way to recognize him/her and to formally say thank you.

You can be sure that those board members who elect to make a planned gift to your organization will be much more qualified to encourage others to consider establishing planned gifts as well.

Courting the Wealthy, Second Edition.
Edited by Scott C. Stevenson.
© 2010 Stevenson, Inc. Published 2010 by Stevenson, Inc.

Varied Communications That Serve to Cultivate

The highest, most personal level of cultivation is the result of face-to-face contact, but there are additional relationship-building measures you can take through correspondence and printed communications: personal letters and cards, proposals, brochures and newsletters and more. These supplemental forms of communication help to vary the ways in which you can build and strengthen relationships with would-be donors.

Use Your Newsletter to Float Funding Possibilities

To bolster interest in major gifts, produce a regular insiders' report for major donor prospects. Include these and other elements to generate reader interest:

1. Float a small handful of funding ideas in each issue of your report — those that address elements of your strategic plan. Offer a variety of project types: capital, endowment, programming and equipment.

2. Give updates on gifts that were made some time ago to illustrate their lasting impact on your organization and those you serve.

3. Include brief profiles about ordinary persons — teachers, librarians and others — who have made extraordinary gifts. These profiles help other ordinary individuals realize that they, too, can be extraordinarily philanthropic.

Share Your Strategic Plan's Progress With Donors

Gallaudet University (Washington D.C.), which serves deaf and hard-of-hearing undergraduate students, recently adopted a five-year strategic plan — Vision 2020: A Bold Vision For a Bright Future.

The plan includes three major elements: The Vision, Guiding Principles, and Goals and Strategies.

Implementation of the plan began in fall 2009 and focused on strategies related to enrollment and the improvement of graduation rates, says Richard Lytle, special assistant to the president and executive director of strategic planning. Full implementation began in January 2010, around the same time that the university hired a new president.

"So far, most of the sharing of the strategic plan has been internal and among our alumni," says Lytle.

In addition to posting the strategic plan and progress updates on a special strategic planning section of the university's website (http://planning.gallaudet.edu/), Gallaudet officials have communicated the plan and its progress to donors through gift acknowledgements, stewardship reports and articles in their magazine, says Marilyn Lucas, executive director of development.

While university officials have yet to translate the plan into the university's fundraising goals, Lucas says they will be working on doing so in the coming months.

"We still need to identify which fundraising priorities will come out of the strategic plan," the executive director of development notes. "So far, we have worked with the leaders of each of our strategic plan's goals to conduct an internal review of what our priorities will be and how that will evolve into fundraising opportunities."

Sharing the plan with donors has several benefits, says Lucas, including the ability to gain donor perspective on what the university is doing, and how well that is being communicated to donors. "It's a great way to engage people, and engagement helps them see the impact of giving on our institution, which makes them more interested in being a part

of it," she says.

Plans are for the university's new president, T. Alan Hurwitz, to eventually work with Lucas and the chief academic officer to identify priorities in the plan appropriate for external funding.

"Dr. Hurwitz came from the deaf community and has an excellent understanding of our university and its mission," says Lytle. "He is very knowledgeable about, and committed to, the strategic plan."

Hiring a new president at the same time as implementing a new strategic plan presents a fabulous opportunity to share the plan with external audiences, says Lucas: "Sharing the plan is a terrific way to get him out in front of donors."

In preparation for developing fundraising goals around the strategic plan's priorities, the university has been rebuilding its development program, hiring Lucas in June 2009, and launching a new major gift and planned giving program in September 2009. "We're working on identifying top prospects that the president should see first," she says. "We're looking at our six-figure and above prospects and going through them one by one to determine our first move and get our new president in to meet as many as possible."

Some of the ways they will be doing that, and communicating their strategic plan in the process, include:

- Breakfast meetings with donors.
- A letter from the president with personalized notes to all donors of $1,000 and up, introducing himself and communicating his excitement about the plan with them.
- A letter from the president to those who have not yet made gifts, introducing himself, and encouraging them to be part of the university's promising future.

Sources: Marilyn Lucas, Executive Director of Development; Richard Lytle, Special Assistant to the President and Executive Director of Strategic Planning; Gallaudet University, Washington, D.C. Phone (202) 651-5410 (Lucas) or (202) 651-5894 (Lytle). E-mail: marilyn.lucas@gallaudet.edu or Richard.lytle@gallaudet.edu

Engage Donors, Volunteers by Sharing Response Cards by Mail and in Person

Bounce-back for someone who may be a candidate for establishing a scholarship.

Name _____
Address_____
City/ST/ZIP _____ __ __
Work Phone (_____) _____
Cell/Home Phone (_____)_____
E-mail _____
Occupation _____
Title _____

I would like to learn more about establishing or adding to a named scholarship. Please provide me with additional information on the following topic(s):

- ○ How scholarships help students.
- ○ How scholarships help the college.
- ○ How scholarships help our society.
- ○ How to establish a named scholarship.
- ○ Using memorial gifts to establish a scholarship.
- ○ Annual scholarships and how they work.
- ○ Endowed scholarships and how they work.
- ○ Placing restrictions on scholarships.
- ○ Establishing or adding to a scholarship through my estate.
- ○ Selection of scholarship recipients.
- ○ Meeting the recipients of my scholarship.
- ○ Potential tax benefits of establishing a scholarship.

Every face-to-face or direct mail contact you have with people should allow you to invite their involvement with your organization in some way. Whether meeting with a first-time or long-time donor, the person's growing involvement with your cause is the single most important factor in generating gifts, volunteer assistance or both.

So what systems do you have in place that help show you when someone may be interested? How do you know when someone might want to establish a scholarship? Get involved in planning a special event? Step up to assist in your capital campaign?

Put response cards or bounce backs to work to help you identify person's interest level in various elements of your nonprofit organization. Use them wherever possible. Include a response card with that new brochure. Add a returnable postcard with that donor correspondence. When you meet with anyone, select a response card that best fits the circumstances and share it with the prospect.

The response card gives your contacts a call to action, a tangible reason to get back to you. And when they do, you don't have to guess or read minds. You have evidence that they have expressed interest in learning more about some aspect of your organization and perhaps, how they can assist your efforts.

As you can see from the examples here, there is no limit to ways you can use this simple tool. Assess the many ways in which bounce backs may be useful in your work.

Bounce-back survey for persons wishing to assist with a special event.

Your special event sounds like fun! Count me in! Please contact me with information on how I can assist you with it in the following way(s):

Name _____
Address_____
City/ST/ZIP _____
Work Phone (_____) _____
Cell or Home Phone (_____)_____
E-mail _____
Occupation & Title _____

- ❑ Attend the event
- ❑ Chair or co-chair a committee
- ❑ Help identify/secure sponsors
- ❑ Chair or co-chair event
- ❑ Assist with ticket sales
- ❑ Assist with location and design
- ❑ Assist with publicity
- ❑ Recruit volunteers

Name _____
Address_____
City/ST/ZIP _____
Work Phone (_____) _____
Cell or Home Phone (_____)_____
E-mail _____
Occupation & Title _____

Please contact me! I'm interested in learning more about the following:

- ○ The college's history and mission.
- ○ Distinguishing achievements of the college.
- ○ Course offerings/majors.
- ○ Career advising.
- ○ Financial aid/scholarship assistance.
- ○ Upcoming calendar of events.
- ○ Speakers bureau topics.
- ○ Volunteer opportunities.
- ○ Exploring planned gift opportunities.
- ○ Annual fund opportunities.
- ○ Endowed gift opportunities.
- ○ How to establish a scholarship.
- ○ The college's future plans.
- ○ Alumni activities and involvement.
- ○ Distinguished graduates of the institution.
- ○ Status of the endowment.
- ○ Other_____

Return card for persons/businesses who would consider hosting a reception or open house on your organization's behalf.

Name _____
Address_____
City _____ State_____ ZIP _____
Work Phone (_____) _____
Cell or Home Phone (_____)_____
E-mail _____
Occupation _____
Title _____

I'm interested in learning more about what's involved with hosting a reception or open house. Tell me more about:

- ❑ Purpose of hosting receptions/open houses.
- ❑ Range of involvement/responsibilities.
- ❑ Who does what — staff vs. host responsibilities.
- ❑ Where to host an event — home vs. another location.
- ❑ Who has hosted events in the past.
- ❑ Examples of successful receptions and open houses your organization has hosted in the past.
- ❑ Examples of what past events have accomplished.

Educate Donors and Would-be Donors to Effectively Market Endowment Gifts

This article, on the giving website for Syracuse University (Syracuse, NY), helps donors and would-be donors better understand endowment gifts:

How an Endowment Gift Works

In this step-by-step illustration, you'll see how an endowment gift works, and the benefits that accrue to SU, our students and the donor.

1. A College of Visual and Performing Arts alumna makes a $50,000 gift (the minimum amount required) to the Setnor School of Music to establish a named endowed scholarship in memory of her father.

2. A gift agreement is drafted between Syracuse University and the donor, guaranteeing that her gift will be added to The Syracuse Endowment and used solely for its stated purpose.

3. The donor's named scholarship fund buys units in The Syracuse Endowment, much as one buys shares in a mutual fund.

4. The Board of Trustees' Investment and Endowment Committee prudently invests the donor's gift across major asset classes in the University's portfolio to maximize long-term total return, within acceptable levels of risk.

5. A predetermined portion of the annual return (currently calculated as 4.4 percent of the average market value during the previous three fiscal years) is used to provide a scholarship for one music student per year. The fund's principal remains intact.

6. The remainder of the annual return is reinvested in the named fund's principal as a hedge against inflation and to generate growth.

7. The named fund continues to grow, ensuring future scholarship support.

As you can see, the advantages of an endowed fund are many. A talented musician receives financial support. The Setnor School of Music is able to use the scholarship to recruit and retain top students. A steady revenue stream allows the school to plan for future needs. And the donor has created a living legacy.

The example here is just one of the many ways endowment gifts can have an impact. In addition to scholarships, donors can endow faculty chairs or professorships or support academic programs, student activities, the library, athletics or other programs or departments.

To learn more about creating an endowment with an outright gift, a pledge or a bequest, contact us.

The giving website for Syracuse University (Syracuse, NY) offers a step-by-step illustration of how an endowment gift works.

Brian C. Sischo, vice president for development, says they developed the illustration because they found many donors did not understand or misunderstood the potential impact of their endowment gift. "It's been a useful tool," he says. "Particularly in light of the market, some donors don't understand the difference between book value and market value. Having a guide that takes them through the steps prevents issues later on."

Sischo says they don't use the illustration in the solicitation process, but rather as a source of information for donors considering an endowment gift, as a post-gift follow-up tool to answer donor questions and as an appendix in endowment stewardship reports.

Syracuse's How an Endowment Gift Works website illustration is shown at left.

Source: Brian C. Sischo, Vice President for Development, Syracuse University, Syracuse, NY. Phone (315) 443-5466. E-mail: bcsischo@syr.edu

Officials at Syracuse University (Syracuse, NY) share this sample endowment agreement to help prospective donors better understand the endowment gift process.

Content not available in this edition

Connect With Donors Through Multiple Sources

Have more than one communication channel with a prospect — the CEO, development officer, board member — so if the prospect severs ties with one, his/her ties to your organization remain intact.

Celebrate Gift Anniversary

Do you have a list of donor names and dates identifying when significant gifts were made to your nonprofit?

Go through past records to prepare a list of donors and the dates of their gifts. Then, on the anniversary of each gift, send a letter to the donor (or children of the donor), reminding them of the gift and describing the impact it has made and is making in your organization.

Your appreciation won't go unnoticed.

Develop a Well-thought-out Endowment Handout

To show would-be donors that you are serious about the importance of gifts to your endowment, take the time to develop an attractive and comprehensive brochure that covers key components of endowment giving.

The content of your brochure or booklet may include but not be limited to:

✓ **List of existing named funds** — This list, which may include photos of the donors, serves as a great marketing tool in two respects: It motivates would-be donors to establish funds of their own and it recognizes existing donors and encourages them to add to their funds.

✓ **Examples of endowment's impact** — How is your current endowment positively impacting your organization and those you serve? How are individual named endowments making a difference?

✓ **A list of named fund opportunities** — A wish list of available opportunities that, along with the minimum cost of establishing each fund, gives donors choices and can help pinpoint funding interests.

✓ **Endowment history and performance** — Use the handout as an opportunity to educate the public about your endowment. Informed individuals are more likely to make a significant investment.

✓ **Benchmarking goals** — Don't hesitate to compare your endowment to similar organizations to which you aspire. Use charts to illustrate differences between your charity's and others' endowments.

✓ **Biographical information about your investment committee and endowment manager** — Show would-be donors that their gifts will be well-stewarded by respected and competent individuals.

✓ **Strategic plan summary** — Summarize those portions of your strategic plan that help substantiate the importance of a growing endowment.

✓ **Description of types of gifts used to establish named endowments** — Describe the various ways in which endowment gifts can be funded (e.g., cash, securities, property). Also distinguish between outright and various types of planned gifts (e.g., bequests, charitable gift annuities).

✓ **Testimonials** — Incorporate some testimonials from those who have established endowment funds. These brief quotes may be included in your list of existing funds.

✓ **Organizational achievements** — People want to know they are investing with a winner. Share specific achievements your charity has made in recent years. List ways that demonstrate you are a good steward of their gifts (e.g., number of consecutive years of balanced budgets).

✓ **Action steps** — Point out the steps anyone can take to explore endowment gifts. Whom do they contact? Stress the confidentiality of all inquiries.

Offer A-to-Z Gift Choices

To convey to prospective donors the broad range of giving opportunities available in an easy-to-use format, the University of Colorado Foundation (Boulder, CO) offers a searchable and browsable A-to-Z list of 600 of the foundation's 2,000 funds. Posted only on the foundation's website, the list is regularly updated with new opportunities.

The list illustrates the diversity of work going on at the university and its four campuses and inspires prospective donors to see how our work connects with their passion, says Jeremy Simon, foundation spokesperson. "We didn't want to curtail the number of giving opportunities offered online. We decided to err on the side of inclusion."

Simon says that while they want prospective donors to see all giving opportunities, they recognize that not all donors want so much information. They are revising their Give Now link, which currently goes directly to the full alphabetical listing, to include only selected broad and high-priority giving opportunities and a link to the full list.

View the Foundation's A-to-Z listing of giving opportunities at www.cufund.org/giving-opportunities/a-z-listing.

Source: Jeremy Simon, Spokesperson, University of Colorado Foundation, Boulder, CO. Phone (303) 541-1218. E-mail: Jeremy.simon@cufund.org

Share Construction Updates With Donors, Would-be Donors

During the construction of a new student residence and dining commons at Bates College (Lewiston, ME), Doug Hubley of the college's office of communications and media relations wrote regular updates on the progress of the construction.

To share Hubley's observations, staff posted his construction updates on the college's news home page (www.bates.edu/x165427.xml) at least once a month throughout the construction that began in 2006 and ended in 2008, sometimes more frequently if developments warranted, says Bryan McNulty, director of communications and media relations.

A campus construction update also served as an anchored feature in every BatesNews, a monthly e-newsletter sent to about 21,000 alumni, parents and friends, and copied to all faculty and staff.

"These updates became popular with readers," says McNulty. "Doug wrote them with his own voice and developed a following of folks who looked forward both to his information and wry humor in photo captions and salted through the text."

The goals of the campus construction updates, McNulty says, were to:

✓ Generate interest and excitement in the college's major physical improvements (a key message).

✓ Show how the construction relates to a campus facilities master plan. Message: Bates is a strategic and careful steward.

✓ Engage with alumni, potential donors.

✓ Keep the campus community in the know on developments related to the college's major construction projects.

To encourage engagement, Hubley ended each update with the following line, which helped elicit queries and comments: "Can we talk? What do you think about the campus improvements process? What do you know that we don't? We want to hear from you. Please e-mail your questions and comments to: Doug Hubley (link to his e-mail address) with 'Construction Update' in the subject line."

Check out an online archive of Hubley's campus construction updates at: www.bates.edu/campus-improvements.xml

Source: Bryan McNulty, Director, Communications and Media Relations, Bates College, Lewiston, ME. Phone (207) 786-6330. E-mail: bmcnulty@bates.edu

Calendar-themed Donor Report Stands Out Year-round

Design a 12-month calendar to serve as your annual donor report, using photos and brief copy to showcase areas in which donors have made an impact.

Such a report is more likely than a traditional report to be kept and displayed throughout the year, serving as a daily reminder of the many good things your organization accomplishes.

Officials at the University of San Diego (San Diego, CA) have used this format for their president's report for three years, says Julene Snyder, senior director of communications. "Choosing an overarching theme for each (year's calendar) has allowed us to produce pieces that have a cohesive and distinctive look."

Snyder says recipients report they use the calendar reports all year, and appreciate the calendar's beauty and practicality.

When developing each year's concept, Snyder's creative team involves the university president early in the process. That way they can be sure the report clearly reflects the president's priorities for the institution, Snyder emphasized. "We also make sure that as many voices as possible are included," she added. "From students to deans, faculty to alumni, parents to administrators, we solicit quotes about the University of San Diego and weave them into our narrative so that as many constituents as possible feel a sense of ownership."

View the university's 2009 president's report, which was created as a 2010 desk calendar, at: www.sandiego.edu/publications/presidentsreport2009/

Source: Julene Snyder, Senior Director, Communications, University of San Diego, San Diego, CA. Phone (619) 260-4684. E-mail: julene@sandiego.edu. Website: www.sandiego.edu

Use Existing Endowments to Cultivate New Endowment Donors

One way to cultivate new endowment donors is to showcase your current endowment donors, says J. Richard Ely, Jr., owner, Strategic Fundraising Consultants (Providence, RI).

"Generate a list that shows all of your endowment funds so that prospective donors can see that you have endowment funds that go back many years," Ely says. "Prospective donors can get a sense that you are keeping faith with donors."

For example, Ely says, showing that you are still honoring a 1922 donor's gift to purchase books for science tells donors you are good stewards of donors' gifts.

When you meet with donors, Ely says, show them this list and say, "Look at this list of distinguished people you are joining when you create an endowment fund."

Source: J. Richard Ely, Jr., Owner, Strategic Fundraising Consultants, Providence, RI. Phone (401) 274-3863. E-mail: rely@planned-giving.com

Donor Recognition as a Form of Cultivation

Appropriate donor recognition should accompany each and every gift, regardless of any subsequent gifts that may be realized. And yet, that level of genuine recognition can play a role in future gifts. Recognition and stewardship comprise the circle of giving that can begin the cycle of giving over again.

Don't Underestimate the Power of a Donor Wall

You might not think a prominently displayed donor wall that lists major donors' names would provide much incentive for others to give. But it does.

Be sure all marketing efforts state that anyone who gives above a certain level will have his/her name(s) listed on a handsome donor wall to be permanently displayed in a prominent location.

Consider going a step further to say that names will be categorized into three levels of giving.

Although a permanent display in and of itself may not motivate a major gift, it can influence someone's decision to give generously, and it serves as a great way to recognize donors who make principal gifts.

Engage Donor's Family in Recognition Efforts

When an individual or couple makes a major gift, ask for permission to involve their adult children in recognizing the gift. Doing so will serve as an important first step in cultivating those heirs to one day make similar gifts or to add to an existing family gift.

You can involve a donor's family by:

1. Inviting input on ways their parents might be recognized. Share some recognition options on which they can comment.

2. Making sure the entire family gets VIP treatment during any recognition events or ceremonies that take place: seating, public introductions and more.

3. Including the children in ongoing stewardship efforts: periodic reports on the impact of their parent's gift, invitations to your organization's events and so forth.

Calendar Thanks Donors, Recognizes Constituents

Some promotional tools do double duty.

For example, staff with James Madison University's office of advancement (Harrisonburg, VA) developed the Be the Change calendar to coincide with the university's Be the Change campaign, launched in 2006. The calendar celebrates persons making a difference while thanking donors.

"The calendar promotes the university's alumni, faculty and students who are making a difference in the world," says Theresa Lind, events coordinator. "It illuminates how these people arm themselves with the power of knowledge, as Madison did, to change the world for the better."

Distributed since the campaign's launch, the 4 1/2 X 5 1/2-inch calendars are given at the university's scholarship luncheon, regional campaign events and given to various donors by development officers, alumni, faculty and staff.

Persons wishing to nominate someone for the calendar can complete a nomination form online (www.jmu.edu/bethechange) or with a calendar insert. Nominations must explain how the person has made a difference, how he/she made a contribution to Be the Change, plus the nominee's name, address and affiliation with the university.

A committee in the communications, marketing and public affairs office reviews nominations and selects persons to appear on the calendar pages.

Content not available in this edition

Source: Theresa Lind, Events Coordinator, James Madison University, Harrisburg, VA.
Phone (540) 568-8867. E-mail: lindtl@jmu.edu

Create Donor Photo Books

For a unique major donor gift, create a book with photos of a special event, building project or constituents using your facilities and/or programs.

For instance, a hardcover, 20-page, 8-1/2 X 11-inch book from Shutterfly (www.shutterfly.com) costs under $35.

"You could use the same photos for each book, but personalize the text for each donor," says Allie Smith, donor relations coordinator, Oregon Food Bank (Portland, OR). "With one click, you could also create a softcover 5 X 7-inch version of the same book for $10 to $15."

For a more personal connection, leave space next to each photo for clients to write personal messages.

Additional photo book websites:

✓ www.Kodakgallery.com — Click "Shop," then "Photo Books"

✓ www.Lulu.com — Click "Publish," then "Photo Books"

✓ www.mypublisher.com

✓ www.picaboo.com

✓ www.photobookmemories.com

Source: Allie Smith, Donor Relations Coordinator, Oregon Food Bank, Portland, OR. Phone (503) 282-0555, ext. 283. E-mail: Asmith@oregonfoodbank.org

Four Ways to Express Heartfelt Appreciation on a Budget

When it's time to pay special tribute to someone highly important to your organization, remember that some of the most meaningful gifts of appreciation are those that require creativity, time and input from a variety of people, but not necessarily a lot of cash.

Chances are the person you are honoring already has a wall filled with plaques, inscribed crystal paperweights and engraved silver bowls. Rather than looking to add to this collection, seek instead a way to create a more meaningful form of recognition.

Here are ideas to get you started on your personalized recognition:

Make a 'This is Your Life' Video

Create and produce an amateur video of your honoree's life featuring highlights of involvement in your organization. Interview friends, volunteers, administrators, board members and others whose lives have been touched in a positive way. Show results of projects the honoree has helped complete and the impact those projects have had on persons your organization serves. Include video of photos of the honoree in a candid moment, or working with others — but let the honoree believe it's for another purpose until you are ready to screen your production.

Create a Commemorative Work of Art

If you have a skilled artist among your volunteer base, ask the person to draw a portrait of the honoree as part of a collage spotlighting his or her accomplishments for your organization. Invest in quality framing so the recipient will be proud to display it.

Or you may wish to create a simpler but equally heartfelt project. Gather young artists (children you serve, or children of your staff or volunteers) to paint a large mural to present to your honored supporter. You also can ask them to paint individual works following a theme, then assemble and present the works in a large bound book.

Another idea: Engage talented adult volunteers to create a group project, such as a set of holiday ornaments, hand-painted glassware or beautiful needlepoint. If they sew, each could create a square for a colorful quilt.

Make a Memory Book

Buy a large, well-made scrapbook (with room for additional pages) and fill with photos, mementos such as event programs, ribbons, badges, news clippings and special items to provide a timeline of your honoree's involvement. Ask friends and family to help locate photos.

Chances are several of your volunteers are quite skilled at scrapbooking and would be happy to create a multi-paged work of art for your honoree using the many themed stickers, picture anchors and creative papers available.

Ask everyone in your organization who knows the honoree to sign the book, and even write messages of congratulations and appreciation, high school yearbook-style.

Give Special Donors Their Own Special Day

Make a proclamation to hold an annual Pat Johnson Day at your institution on a date that is important to your honoree. Have your chief executive officer, board members and other appropriate officials and even your mayor sign the certificate. To add even more meaning, mark that special day as an annual date for your institution to do something meaningful in the recipient's honor, like begin an annual campaign, host a luncheon or start a canned food drive.

Create Policy for Publicizing Momentous Gifts As First Step in Stewarding Donors

Take inspiration from these two organizations to publicize your next major gift:

Share Announcement With Those Who Will Benefit From It Most

Washburn University (Topeka, KS) recently received its largest single gift from an individual — a $5 million gift from Trish and Richard Davidson to supplement faculty salaries in its School of Business.

To publicize the momentous gift, Washburn officials turned to the university policy that calls for all gift announcements to be structured to the donor's specifications, says Wendy Walker Zeller, director of donor relations and communications for the Washburn Endowment Association, Washburn University's fundraising arm.

The Davidsons wanted to be present for this gift announcement, Zeller says, "so we spent a great deal of time working out the details to meet their wishes." The Davidsons asked to speak to a class of business students. Also attending the class? The news media, along with the university president, endowment association president, business school dean and board of regents chair. The 100-some students were invited to stay for the gift announcement, which took place just after the press arrived in the classroom.

Media received press packets featuring the Davidsons' biographies and were seated at the front of the classroom. A backdrop with the university logo and drape displaying the business school were arranged for the announcement.

"The students gave a spontaneous standing ovation following the announcement, which was filmed by a couple of the local TV stations," she says.

Following the gift announcement, says Zeller, the media were invited to interview the donors in a separate location against a backdrop of the university logo.

"Other than a few people on campus and several trustees, we kept the gift amount and identity of the donors under wraps until the official announcement, which helped build suspense and pique press interest," she says. She plans to include an article about the gift in the endowment's annual report and the next issue of the alumni magazine.

Carefully Time Release of News to Maximize Publicity, Impact

Chatham Hall (Chatham, VA), an independent college preparatory high school for girls, recently received a $31 million gift from the estate of Elizabeth Beckwith Nilsen, a former student. The gift was the largest single gift to any girls' independent school.

Because of the magnitude of the gift, Melissa Evans Fountain, director of the office of advancement, says they followed this special plan of action in publicizing it:

On announcement day, classes were delayed until 9:30 a.m. From 8 to 9 a.m., the president of the board and head of school announced the gift to the faculty and answered questions about the gift. At 9 a.m., faculty were joined by the staff and students, and the head of school and board president announced the gift to this larger group.

Staff sent a news release at 9:15 a.m. through US 1 Premium Newswire, the Philanthropy Microlist and the Education Microlist and posted it on the school's website.

At 9:30 a.m., after the all-school meeting, the head of Chatham Hall sent an e-mail announcing the gift to all major educational associations, suggesting they share the news with their constituents.

From 9:30 to 10:30 a.m., calls were made to members of the Alumnae Council and Parent Advisory Council, past heads of the school, certain major donors and other VIPs (all trustees and several top donors knew about the gift prior to the announcement).

At 10:30 a.m. an e-mail blast was sent to all constituents in the school's database and the announcement was posted on the school's Facebook page.

That same day, college officials mailed a press release to donor prospects (alumnae, parents and friends) with a cover letter announcing the gift in the context of the school's capital campaign. They also sent the press release to state and local VIPs, area leaders in the Episcopal Church (with which the college is affiliated) and to those on an admission office list that included prospective students and educational consultants. A special article was also written for the school's fall 2009 alumnae magazine.

Sources: Melissa Evans Fountain, Director of the Office of Advancement, Chatham Hall, Chatham, VA. Phone (434) 432-5549. E-mail: mfountain@chathamhall.org
Wendy Walker Zeller, Director of Donor Relations & Communications, Washburn Endowment Association, Topeka, KS. Phone (785) 670-4483. E-mail: wwalker@wea.org

Focus on Donors Individually When Recognizing Major Gifts

Q. *We are holding an event at which we will be recognizing two donors, one who gave $1 million, and one who gave $100,000. How do we recognize both donors appropriately at the same event?*

"Hold separate recognition ceremonies that feature each donor. You wouldn't want to have the ceremonies at the same time because it would mean both donors would be sharing the spotlight, which wouldn't be in the best interest of the donor who gave the larger amount. If you have to hold the ceremonies at the same time, you might want to host a private luncheon or dinner with the president and the $1 million donor and his or her family either before or following the event. This elevates the larger donor's generosity to a higher level. The lower-level donor could be invited to a luncheon or dinner with the dean of the school benefiting from the gift."

— *Leanne Poon, Manager, Donor Relations & Stewardship, University of British Columbia (Vancouver, British Columbia, Canada)*

"Dollar level alone cannot decide the course of action. At either of those donation levels, you should have some idea of the relationship of gift size to potential as well as what's most meaningful to and in keeping with the personality of the donor.

"The $100,000 gift might have been an extreme stretch for that donor, the most they can ever give. The $1 million gift might have been a moderate or even 'typical' gift for the other donor. Each donor knows which category he or she is in. If the smaller gift was a stretch gift and the larger donor gets more recognition, what message does that convey about the values of your organization?

"There are more folks out there who might be able to consider a $100,000 gift — even as a stretch gift — under certain circumstances than a $1 million gift. Don't make the prize too out of reach for them."

— *Mary Kay Filter Dietrich, Vice President for Development & External Relations, Urban League of Greater Pittsburgh (Pittsburgh, PA)*

Recognizing Your Top Donor

Q. *"What do you do to recognize your most significant donor in a significant way?"*

"At the American Diabetes Association and with our Research Foundation, we have a standard set of recognition opportunities (personal tours during our scientific sessions, names in annual reports and ads in our consumer publication, "Diabetes Forecast"). But what makes our stewardship unique is that our stewardship director will discuss with our staff member and our donor ways that are meaningful to him or her. For example, we don't own a building, but we do have research grants that can be named in honor of the donor. Then each time the researcher is published, we give the donor copies of the article. We will also arrange personal lab tours at private gatherings for the donor and the scientists."

— *Elly Brtva, Managing Director of Individual Gifts, American Diabetes Association (Alexandria, VA)*

"This past year, the office of medical development raised several endowed professorships (each professorship is a $4 million gift). At a small dinner of about 50 people hosted by the dean of the medical school, we recognize the donor and the faculty who will be the chair holder. The donor and faculty member each received a professorship medal and Stanford chair in addition to professionally designed photo albums commemorating the evening."

— *Lorraine Alexander, Senior Director of Development, Neuroscience Institute, Stanford University (Menlo Park, CA)*

"The Minneapolis Institute of Arts has a long-time trustee and major benefactor who has made countless gifts over his lifetime. During the opening of our new wing, we honored him and his legacy of support by announcing a permanent art endowment in his name. His fellow trustees had contributed nearly $4 million to this art endowment as a tribute to his decades of generosity.

"As a result, the museum — and the community — now have a permanent testament to this donor's commitment to excellence in our collections."

— *Joan Grathwol Olson, Director of Development, The Minneapolis Institute of Arts (Minneapolis, MN)*

Appropriate Gifts to Say Thanks to Foundations

Q: *We would like to thank our foundation donors for their recent grants to our organization. What type of gifts do foundations prefer to receive?*

"Frequently, development-oriented people react to foundation giving with an individual giving mindset rather than a foundation mindset. Unless it's a small family foundation — which is often just a vehicle by which individuals are doing their personal giving — this doesn't work. At my first foundation relations job, as early as the interview process it became apparent to me that the top folks in development did not understand that foundation giving works differently than individual giving. It's important to match the mode of thanks to the motivation for giving — individuals like personal recognition, corporations like visibility and foundations like knowing they've done good. A sincere letter of thanks and a press release, which you have cleared with the foundation, usually takes care of that!"

— Deborah S. Koch, Director of Grants, Springfield Technical Community College (Springfield, MA)

"It depends on the foundation, of course. Recently, we did something that worked well for one of our major foundation donors. The foundation had been giving to us a yearly grant to be used for scholarships for 28 years. We contacted all of the previous student recipients and asked them to write a letter of thanks to the foundation. About 20 students responded with wonderful letters of where they are now and how the scholarship helped them achieve their goals. We then put the letters together with a recent picture and their yearbook picture in a Snapfish photo book. The foundation loved it! We also kept a copy for the development office and use it when we meet with prospective donors to show the impact of scholarships on our students."

— Suzanne Libenson, Director of Foundation Relations and Government Funding, Holy Family University (Philadelphia, PA)

"Because we're a small, private institution, we try not to be too extravagant when it comes to donor recognition. All donors, including foundation donors, receive an official thank-you letter from our president. I also handwrite a note to our foundation donors and call them if I happen to know someone at the foundation. If the grant is for student scholarships, students will also write thank-you letters to the foundation. Foundation donors are also recognized on our outdoor donor recognition wall, on giving society plaques in our administration building and in the college's online annual Honor Roll of Donors."

— Cindy C. Godwin, Director of Development, Meredith College (Raleigh, NC)

Donor Recognition Idea

Have you ever considered using your organization's board meetings as a way to recognize key donors' generous gifts?

Make a point to invite recent donors to be introduced and perhaps make a brief address at each meeting. Doing so provides a special kind of donor recognition and also emphasizes the importance of principal giving among board members and staff.

Cultivation Technique

■ Don't miss an opportunity to publicize names of donors and would-be donors to establish a public connection between them and your charity: lists of those who have attended your special event in a thank-you ad placed in the local newspaper, lists of new members in your newsletter and so forth.

An Idea Worth Repeating

The idea is certainly not new, but because it works, it's worth repeating:

Make a point to review newspapers, business journals, local and regional magazines and other publications that publish job promotions, weddings, anniversaries and other positive happenings that focus on individual persons or businesses.

Cut out announcements and send them to the persons or business owners with an appropriate note of congratulations and a business card. You may even consider laminating the article to provide a well-preserved memento to the recipient.

Such from-the-heart gestures can go a long way in the cultivation process.

Courting the Wealthy, Second Edition.
Edited by Scott C. Stevenson.
© 2010 Stevenson, Inc. Published 2010 by Stevenson, Inc.

Stewardship as a Form of Cultivation

The act of stewarding existing donors – continually sharing the impact of their gifts – also serves as a way to cultivate additional gifts. Although ongoing acts of stewardship should accompany any major gifts, regardless of any future gifts, a well satisfied donor is much more likely to make subsequent gifts at some point.

Develop Individualized Stewardship Techniques

How can you update your current stewardship techniques to better serve your major donors and attract new major gifts?

At the California Institute of the Arts (CalArts), Valencia, CA, officials recently revised donor stewardship methods by eliminating many membership benefits and turning the focus instead on individualized stewardship of its leadership annual donors.

"Our higher-level donors had been receiving an increasing number of invitations to special events," says Brigid Slipka, director of annual giving programs. "This benefits structure was building too much of a quid-pro-quo culture instead of cultivating donors who wished to support the well-being of our school. Some donors were telling us that they would no longer give because they could not come to the events. On the other end of the spectrum, donors who were invested in the school weren't as interested in a benefit as they were in a deep connection to the mission of CalArts."

Also, Slipka says, because there were so many donor variables — residence (often far from the Los Angeles area where the events were held), ways in which they were connected to CalArts, and their personal interests — creating one set of benefits that appealed to all of them would be virtually impossible.

"In collaboration with our major gift officers, we now communicate one-on-one with our leadership donors," she says. "We take the opportunity to thank them and directly ask them why they are interested in CalArts and what is most important to them."

From this, they can craft personalized stewardship for each donor, says Slipka. For example, parents of theater students may join the school's president for an intimate reception before a student performance that involves their child, or an alumnus from the animation program interested in high school arts education can show his film to participants of the school's youth education program.

"In addition to meeting the individual interests of the donor, this process also allows for a personal relationship between each donor and development officer," she says. "Building this personal relationship is key in cultivating the next gift."

CalArts still holds a small number of events for donors and prospects, an effort that continues to engage long-time donors while at the same time allowing development staff the flexibility to invite those donors they are still cultivating, says Slipka.

"This way of stewarding donors takes a lot of coordination and double-checking behind the scenes to be sure that donors aren't being contacted from multiple sides or neglected altogether," she says. "Our plan, however, is to save time and energy needed in creating several elaborate events and instead dedicate it toward building personal connections between donors and CalArts."

Source: Brigid Slipka, Director, Annual Giving Programs, California Institute of the Arts, Valencia, CA.
Phone (661) 253-7736. E-mail: bslipka@calarts.edu

Key Stewardship Relations Practices

Each profession has unique customer relations principles. To excel in the fundraising profession, adhere to these practical tips for maintaining good stewardship practices:

- Acknowledge all gifts within 48 hours in the most personalized manner possible.
- Send letters to prospects confirming appointment times and the visit's purpose.
- Follow up visits with a letter summarizing key points and confirming next steps.
- Show that donors' gifts are being used as intended by giving progress reports, tours, etc.
- Confirm how a donor wishes to have his/her name listed in your annual report.
- Thank a donor seven times — in different ways — before asking for another gift.
- Include both spouses in the solicitation process.
- Avoid doing end runs to get to the top decision-maker. Follow protocol.
- Be up-front about the time required for an appointment and then stick to it.
- If you are unable to answer an individual's question with confidence, assure him/her you will get the answer, and then make a point to follow up within 48 hours.
- When a donor or prospective donor takes the time to stop by your office — even without an appointment — make every effort to meet with him/her.

Good Stewardship Matters

Who says timeliness and the personal touch don't count?

One retired physician decided he would begin contributing $1,000 annually to his community's two hospitals.

Officials at one hospital foundation were quick to get a personal note of appreciation out the door within 24 hours after receipt of the gift. The other hospital sent a preprinted thank-you postcard several days later.

This pattern of gift acknowledgment was repeated each year the physician gave his gift.

The retired doctor decided to make a $500,000 gift. Guess where it went? That's right. The entire gift went to the hospital that had always followed up with a personal message promptly, and with a personal touch.

Organizations Need to Be Careful Stewards

What steps do you take to inform donors how their gifts have been used?

Donors need to be assured that their gifts will be used for the purposes for which they were given or many of them may become disenchanted with your organization and stop making gifts, says John Taylor, associate vice chancellor for advancement services at North Carolina State University (Raleigh, NC).

"Many donors think that organizations don't spend donated funds in the manner for which they were intended," he says.

This perception, says Taylor, goes back to how donors are being informed about how their gifts are being used. This is exacerbated by the fact that donors are hearing in the news that organizations are misusing donors' funds.

"This could easily be fixed by communicating to donors during the course of the expenditure of the funds how those funds are being used," he says.

Source: John Taylor, Associate Vice Chancellor for Advancement Services, North Carolina State University, Raleigh, NC. Phone (919) 513-2954. E-mail: johntaylor@ncsu.edu

Host an Annual Memorial Event for Employees, Constituents

To honor the memory of those close to your organization — donors, volunteers, employees, board members and others — why not host an annual memorial event that recognizes those who have died during the past year?

Invite loved ones of persons who have passed away, as well as the public, to an hour-long service that pays tribute to persons who had a connection to your organization.

Such an annual service might include:

✓ A printed program listing those who have died during

the past year along with a brief bio of their lives and affiliation with your organization.

✓ Asking the family and friends of each individual to stand and be recognized.

✓ A permanent wall display or memorial book to honor those who have been memorialized in past years.

An annual service such as this shows respect for these individuals' contributions and emphasizes the fact that they were an important part of your nonprofit's extended family.

Invite a Donor to Your Staff Meeting

As part of regular staff meetings, why not invite a donor to come and share insight into a particular topic such as what motivated him/her to make a gift?

Inviting a donor to meet with your staff has multiple benefits, among them:

1. Both staff and donor benefit by being face to face, associating names and faces.

2. What better way to thank a donor than to bring him/her into your office as a special guest offering advice on some topic?

3. This simple stewardship act serves to involve the

donor in a new and different way. His/her presence will provide a greater appreciation of the overall development function and its importance in your organization.

4. Your staff will discover even more about the donor — motivations, likes/dislikes — that will surely be helpful in the realization of future gifts. You may even identify additional ways in which the donor could become involved with your organization.

5. The thoughts and advice shared by the donor may help in future fundraising efforts.

Letter Serves as Stewardship, Cultivation Tool

In light of today's economy, it's becoming increasingly important to talk about your institution's mission and those it serves, says Kenneth L. Converse, vice president for institutional advancement, Buena Vista University (Storm Lake, IA), "We need to do a better job of communicating with our donors about how we are using their dollars."

With this in mind, Converse and his staff recently sent a letter to the 419 donors who made gifts in 2003 to the university's Estelle Siebens Science Center. Signed by the dean of the School of Science, the letter (shown below) thanked donors for their support and highlighted the program's successes.

"We wanted our donors to feel good about what they did," Converse says. "We wrestled with length, but our sense was that those who were interested in reading the letter would get the powerful message we were trying to convey about the impact the new building has had on our students and institution."

This was the first time they had sent a stewardship letter for anything other than an endowed fund, says Converse, who notes he and his staff plan to look at how they might use this stewardship and cultivation strategy with other projects.

"We should have sent the letter sooner, and would have had we thought about it," he admits. "As it was, the timing was about a year off, but the letter was sent out after our first group of students had finished their four years in the program. Everyone on the recipient list had completed their pledge payments."

Source: Kenneth L. Converse, Vice President for Institutional Advancement, Buena Vista University, Storm Lake, IA. Phone (712) 749-2101. E-mail: CONVERSEK@bvu.edu

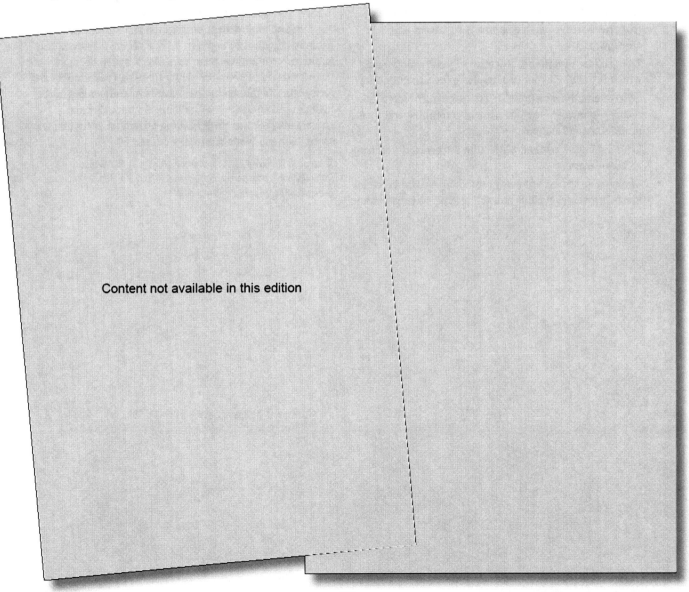

Content not available in this edition

Marketing Endowments Starts With Stewarding Existing Funds

To successfully market your endowment, you need to know and understand what you are marketing and be able to illustrate that understanding to your donor prospects, says J. Richard Ely, Jr., owner of Strategic Fundraising Consultants (Providence, RI).

One of the most effective ways to do so, Ely says, is to work with your board members, chief financial officer, investment committees and others within your organization to create a one-page description of your endowment.

Your endowment description should include:

- A breakdown of the asset allocation in your endowment (stocks, bonds, cash), the amount of each and the grand total.

- A performance analysis that shows how your endowment's assets performed compared to industry averages over time.

- A breakdown of restrictions on the endowment — (e.g., permanently and temporarily restricted and unrestricted).

- The primary investment objective of your endowment, which is based on your endowment's investment policy.

- Who internally is responsible for endowment management — typically, your investment committee and their professional affiliations.

- Who manages your endowment investments, if you have an outside firm.

- The endowment investments custodian — who holds the assets, processes the buy and sell orders, collects income and prepares statements.

"The endowment description shows prospects that you know what you're doing, that you are going to manage their fund into perpetuity, and that you are responsible enough to do that," says Ely.

As a companion piece to your endowment description, it's important to include a list of all of your endowment funds that shows donor prospects you have a long history of careful management of named endowment funds, he says.

"The objection I hear the most from endowment donors is, 'If I give you the money, how do I know it will be used for the purpose I intend it for 50 years from now,'" says Ely. "When donor prospects see an endowment fund on your list that was established in 1922 to purchase science books for your library, for example, and that you are still doing that every year, they will feel confident that if they give you their money, you will do the same for them."

With an endowment description and current endowment list in hand, you can begin to look at all the ways you can publicize your endowment, says Ely. Ways to do so include feature stories in your newsletter that showcase donors and recipients and talk about the benefits of endowment and a listing of all endowment funds in your annual report.

He also recommends holding an annual event that showcases your endowment and its donors.

Source: J. Richard Ely, Jr., Owner, Strategic Fundraising Consultants, Providence, RI. Phone (401) 274-3863. E-mail: rely@planned-giving.com

Content not available in this edition

Engage Major Donors With Capital Project Scrapbook

Looking for a way to steward your capital project donors? Laurie Rogers, director of development, Peter Paul Development Center (Richmond, VA), suggests starting a scrapbook of your building's progress.

Rogers has created a photo scrapbook for the last three capital projects she has been involved with in Richmond. At the groundbreaking, she presents donors with a three-ring binder. She then mails photo updates to them — already three-hole punched — at least once a month.

"I include a note about how things are going," says Rogers. "In this economy, any progress is good progress." Donors unable to attend the groundbreaking receive the binder by mail or personal delivery.

Rogers suggests scheduling hardhat tours once a quarter for donors to see the progress for themselves: "Even if they don't come to campus, they know that you are tending this investment that they have so graciously and generously made in your project," she says. "In all three capital projects I've been involved in, the message has always been the same — gratitude. The donors have been quite appreciative of this effort."

Source: Laurie Rogers, Director of Development, Peter Paul Development Center, Richmond, VA.
Phone (804) 780-1195. E-mail: plrogers@earthlink.net

Include Donors in Post-campaign Success

Just because your capital campaign has successfully concluded doesn't mean the party's over. It's important to share your campaign's success with donors. After all, their generosity made it a success.

Involve donors in your post-campaign period in the following ways:

- Convey appreciation in a personal way through various methods: personal letters from your organization's CEO, campaign chair and others.
- Follow through on naming gifts with appropriate plaques. Check with donors to be sure names are spelled and listed correctly before authorizing the engraving.
- Invite donors to celebrate in the completion of renovated or newly constructed capital projects to which they contributed. Consider a larger, all-inclusive celebration as well as more individualized gatherings.
- For donors who establish named endowment funds, revisit the details of the fund: how annual interest will be used, the agreed-upon name and fund description and such.

Lightning Source UK Ltd.
Milton Keynes UK
UKOW01f0823020813

214783UK00006B/171/P

9 781118 692073